WILD LIFE

AN ANIMAL HISTORY OF AOTEAROA

Philippa Werry

Oratia

PHOTOGRAPH CREDITS: FRONT COVER Tuatara, Neil Fitzgerald. **BACK COVER** (top to bottom) see following pages for information: pp. 84, 18, 69, 61, Tony Foster, Flickr. Title page Giles Laurent, Wikimedia (W); page 4: Sarah Elworthy; p. 7 (top to bottom): 2006-0010-1/37 From the series: Extinct Birds of New Zealand, 2005 by Paul Martinson, Te Papa Tongarewa Museum of New Zealand (Te Papa); John Mason, Department of Conservation NZ (DoC); From *Amphibia and reptiles*, Gadow, Hans, Macmillan and Co., London, New York, 1901; p. 8 Brian Donovan, courtesy of School of Environment, University of Auckland; p. 9 Gavin Mouldey; p. 10 Tom Simpson (left), Canterubry Museum; p. 11 EP/1986/3163/15-F, Alexander Turnbull Library, Wellington (ATL); p. 13 Kirsty Myron (top); TheyLookLikeUs; p. 14 Noah, iNaturalist; p. 16 Auckland Museum (top); KeresH, W; Stewart Nimmo, Development West Coast, W; p. 17 EP/1955/1441-F, ATL (top); Mary Morgan-Richards, W; James O'Hanlon, W; p. 19 Trevor Worthy, Te Papa; p. 20 2006-0010-1/18 From the series: Extinct Birds of New Zealand, 2005 by Paul Martinson, Te Papa; p. 21 Science History Institute, W (top); S.027950 Te Papa; p.22 1967-0028-1, Te Papa; p. 23 1944.78.66, Barker Collection, Canterbury Museum; p. 24 Add.Ms.23920 f.49, British Library; p. 25 Forest and Kim Starr, W (left); C. Lagahetau (CL); p. 26 PAColl-8163-38, ATL; p. 27 Dash Huang, Flickr; p. 28 J.G. Keulemans; p. 30 Allie Caulfield, Flickr; p. 31 Extinct Birds of New Zealand, 2005 by Paul Martinson, Te Papa (both images); p. 33 PA2-1359, ATL (top); IA192/483, Archives New Zealand Mahara o te Kawanatanga (ANZ); p. 34 WA-25130-G, ATL; p. 35 PAColl-5926-15 ATL; p. 36 Matt Binns, Flickr (left); Extinct Birds of New Zealand, 2005 by Paul Martinson, Te Papa; p. 37 Leon Berard, W; p. 38 CL (top); © Stuff; p. 40 Peter Vaughan, Flickr (top); Kathrin and Stefan Marks, Flckr; p. 41 Kathrin and Stefan Marks, Flckr (left); CL; p. 42 Pseudopanax, Wikipedia (top); Bequest of G.V. Hudson 1992-0035-2316, Te Papa (middle); Emily Fountain, W; p. 43 Chris Birmingham, W; p. 44 Hocken Collections (both); p. 45 Maungatautari Ecological Island Trust, W; p. 47 Top of page images, clockwise from left: Uwe Schneehagen, W; Tony Wills, W; Don Horne, W; S. Rae, Flickr; DoC (lower left); George Hudson, 2021-0002-3/16-19, Te Papa; p. 48 Bernard Spragg, Flickr (both); p. 49 C. Knox, W; p. 50 Neil Birrell, W (left); Phil Bishop, W; Kath Walker, DoC, W (lower); p. 51 Kath Walker, DoC, W; p. 52 E-453-f-008, ATL; p. 54 A-478-049, ATL (top left); Benjamin444 W; A100.024, Kenneth John Fix, Puke Ariki; p.55 Gaetan Lee, Flickr; p. 56 Ian Southey; p. 58 Michael Williams, Dreamstime; p. 59 Michael Trotter, www.rarebreeds.co.nz; p. 60 Ross Henry, Dreamstime; p. 61 Tara Swan; p. 62 P1993-01183-028a Hocken Library (left); 1/1-002024-G ATL; p. 63 PUBL-0223-184, ATL (top); P1993-011/3 Hocken Library; p. 64 EPH-PT-16-2 Auckland War Memorial Museum (top); CL; p. 65 J.G. Keulemans, W (left); Vertebrate Zoology Curator, World Museum, National Museum, Liverpool; p. 66 Science Learning Hub – Pokapū Akoranga Pūtaiao, The University of Waikato Te Whare Wānanga o Waikato, www.sciencelearn.org.nz (top); CL; LM002959, Te Papa (lower); p. 67 Hans Wismeijer, Dreamstime; p. 69 PAColl-6348-02, ATL; p. 70 DoC (both); p. 71 J.J. Harrison, W; p. 72 Rhododendrites, W; p. 74 1/2-100198-G, ATL; p. 75 Eph-A-TOURISM-NZ-1935-03-front, ATL; p. 76 AWNS-19100210-04-06, Auckland Libraries Heritage Collections (top); AAQA 6393 H1054 ANZ; p. 77 Michael Trotter www.rarebreeds.co.nz; p. 78 Giles Laurent, W; p. 79 Jason Cheng, Dreamstime; p. 80 Greg O'Beirne, W; p. 82 AWNS-19160203-44-2, Auckland Libraries Heritage Collections; p. 83 EP/1956/2382-F, ATL; p. 84 ACGO 8333 IA1 1234/[25] 1912/3767, ANZ (top); EP/1958/0235-F, ATL; p. 85 AAQT 6539 W3537 Box 53 A44488, ANZ; p. 86 AAQT 6539 W3537 Box 44 A21483, ANZ; p. 87 Benjamin Healley, Museums Victoria; p. 89 C-057-002, ATL; p. 90 1/2-122301-F, ATL; p. 92 Philippa Werry (top); Matt Ward W; p. 94 Siobhan Leachman, W; p. 95 Lawrie M., W (top); Sarah Elworthy; p. 96 Chris Winks, W; p. 97 Desmond W. Helmore, Landcare Research, W (top); CL (both lower); p. 98 Andrew Barclay, Flickr.

All efforts to obtain copyright permission for imagery in this book have been made; any further information can be directed to Oratia Books.

Published by Oratia Books, Oratia Media Ltd, 783 West Coast Road, Oratia, Auckland 0604, New Zealand (www.oratia.co.nz).

ISBN 978-1-99-004298-0

Managing Editor: Carolyn Lagahetau
Designer: Sarah Elworthy

First published 2026

Printed in China

CONTENTS

INTRODUCTION

Aotearoa New Zealand was once covered with forests, ferns, wetlands and grasslands. Birds were everywhere and the forest floor crawled with insects, lizards and worms.

Today we still have some of those creatures, but we also have pets in our houses, livestock on our farms, non-native birds like blackbirds, thrushes and sparrows in our trees and non-native fish like trout in our rivers. We have pests and predators like rabbits and hedgehogs, rats, possums, stoats, ferrets and weasels, nibbling foliage and killing native wildlife.

This book contains stories of arrival of the animals, birds and insects that live here now, or once did but are now extinct. How and when did they get here, how did they survive and thrive — or not — how did they change the environment and what is their future?

GONDWANA AND PRE-HUMAN NEW ZEALAND

Millions of years ago, New Zealand was part of a supercontinent called Gondwana.

Gondwana also contained Africa, South America, India, Australia, New Guinea and Antarctica. Gradually, with the movement of continental plates, the continents shifted and broke away, starting with Africa about 170 million years ago.

About 80–85 million years ago, another land mass separated from Gondwana. Geologists call this Zealandia. Much of it was under the sea, but it included New Caledonia, Norfolk Island, the Chatham Islands, the main and smaller islands of New Zealand and the sub-Antarctic islands.

The land that is now New Zealand took with it a collection of birds, fish, reptiles, insects, invertebrates and plants that lived on Gondwana. It was now very remote from its closest land neighbours and its isolation meant that animal (and plant) life here developed some unique characteristics.

FOSSIL EVIDENCE

Fossil finds give clues about early prehistoric creatures that once lived in Aotearoa. The oldest fossils so far discovered were found in 1948 by 14-year-old Malcolm Simpson, on a geology trip to the Cobb Valley near Motueka. The fossils, inside limestone rock, contained marine creatures called trilobites, around 505 million

Creatures of pre-human New Zealand

- For millions of years, until humans arrived, the only new creatures were ones that could swim or fly here or were blown or carried on floating rafts of vegetation across the ocean.
- If animals hadn't evolved before the separation from Gondwana, and they couldn't fly, swim or be blown here, they were absent, for example, snakes and scorpions.
- The sea was home to marine mammals like seals and whales, but there were no large land mammals, so animals evolved and adapted to an environment free of mammal predators. Birds and insects were safe as they foraged, scurried or built nests on the forest floor. Some creatures, like the moa, Haast's eagle, kākāpō, kiwi, wētā, giant weevils and land snails, grew remarkably large.
- Birds like the takahē might have originally flown here and evolved to be poor fliers or flightless, saving the energy needed for flying.
- Some animals that once lived on Zealandia died out and are only known from fossil records. Others became the ancestors of animals living today. Creatures that trace their lineage back to prehistoric ancestors include tuatara, peripatus/ngāokeoke (velvet worm), geckos, giant wētā, wrens and native frogs.

Haast's eagle, *Hieraaetus moorei*.

Powelliphanta hochstetteri, a species of carnivorous giant land snail.

Tuatara, *Sphenodon punctatus*.

One of the oldest fossils in Aotearoa, discovered by Malcolm Simpson in 1948.

years old. Another important fossil site is at Foulden Maar, an ancient volcano crater lake near Middlemarch in Otago that contains hundreds of fossil species including insects, spiders, fish and eels.

How fossils form

Fossils form when an animal or plant dies and, before it can decompose, gets buried and preserved under ash, mud, sand or other sediment. The fossils can be shells, teeth, bones or prints of feathers or footprints. They might stay buried for millions of years until erosion or other land movements expose them.

Until recently, we knew hardly anything about terrestrial (land) animals that might have lived here between the time of the dinosaurs and the last hundred thousand years when moa and other birds have left bones in caves and swamps. That is changing with exciting finds at Lake Manuherikia, an ancient lake-bed site near St Bathans in Central Otago.

In the 1980s, scientists found plant fossils and bones of waterbirds here, but it wasn't until the early 2000s that scientists from Canterbury Museum, Te Papa Tongarewa and Institute of Geological and Nuclear Sciences started a bigger project. Since then, more than 9000 specimens have been collected and more than 70 species identified, sometimes from slivers of bones or teeth.

These fossils — often the tiniest pieces, fragments of bone that measure 5 cm or less, jumbled together and broken — are providing new evidence about astonishing creatures that once lived here: one-metre-tall parrots, flamingo-like birds, terrestrial turtles, giant burrowing bats and even freshwater crocodilians (the ancestors of today's crocodiles). This would make it the southernmost location that crocodilians have lived. Evidence from fragments of jawbone suggest that there might have been small land mammals, apart from bats, including one known as the 'waddling mouse' that doesn't seem to fit into any other animal group.

Fossil records show that birds and animals have arrived, evolved and died out many times

Impression of what the burrowing bat may have looked like.

LEFT Fossil evidence has revealed a large crocodilian lived in New Zealand.

RIGHT Model of giant penguin.

over millions of years. Scientists have used fossilised tree pollen to show that about 14 million years ago it was significantly warmer than today, but this was followed by an age of global cooling with a worldwide temperature drop of 8°C. Many animals that thrived in the warmth, like crocodiles and turtles, would have perished in the cold.

Fossil records from a site at Waipara Greensand, North Canterbury, are helping scientists to understand more about penguin evolution and how many of their adaptive changes happened right here. The finds include ten ancient penguin species with long dagger-like beaks. One was a giant penguin 1.6 m tall (bigger than today's Emperor penguins).

This area on the Waipara River is where Thomas Cockburn-Hood unearthed the first recorded fossils in New Zealand in 1859, including those of an extinct marine reptile called a plesiosaur.

DINOSAURS

Dinosaurs went extinct worldwide about 65 million years ago. Their existence was discovered only from fossil evidence in the nineteenth century.

Did dinosaurs ever roam this country? We know the answer because of the hard work and persistence of fossil-hunter Joan Wiffen. Not a trained scientist, she became interested after attending a night class on geology. She and her husband Pont and their two children travelled around the country looking at fossil sites, and studied geological survey maps to find possible locations closer to home. To their excitement, one map showed a site marked with 'reptilian bones' in the remote Te Hoe Valley in inland Hawke's Bay.

Joan and Pont set off on their first visit to the Mangahouanga Stream in December 1972. They continued their visits for years. Wiffen taught herself from books how to extract fossils from rocks and boulders and identify them. She found fossil bones of marine reptiles like plesiosaurs, mosasaurs and turtles, and in 1975 she found a vertebra which seemed different from these. Four years later, visiting Australia, she saw a similar vertebra on the desk of palaeontologist Dr Ralph Molnar. She sent him a cast of her specimen and he identified it as the tailbone of a theropod, or carnivorous dinosaur. This was the first indication that dinosaurs had lived here.

Pont and Joan Wiffen piecing together a fossil in 1986.

NATIVE, ENDEMIC AND INTRODUCED

Every native species (or its ancestors) was already here when New Zealand separated from Gondwana, or it has arrived since on its own.

New Zealand has a high percentage of endemic animals because of its long isolation period. More than 90% of insects and all native frogs and reptiles are endemic. There are 91 species of native land birds and 85 are endemic. Because of its island nature and rich marine life, New Zealand also has an unusually high proportion of seabirds (those that get most of their food at sea), and 10% of the world's total seabird species are endemic to this country.

Native A species that occurs naturally in one country, but the same or a closely-related species may also live in other countries.
Endemic A native species unique to its own country and found nowhere else.
Introduced A species brought to a country from elsewhere in the world, either on purpose or accidentally.

BATS/PEKAPEKA

Bats were the only land mammals here when the first humans arrived. Their ancestors were probably blown across from Australia and there would have been millions before human settlement; even in the 1800s there were still big colonies. In Māori culture, pekapeka are recognised as ancient creatures linked to the hōkioi, the mythical bird that flies at night to foretell death or disaster, and has a special role as intermediaries between the world of the living and the spirit world.

The long-tailed bat is more common, and found across the

New Zealand long-tailed bat, *Chalinolobus tuberculatus*.

New Zealand short-tailed bats, *Mystacina tuberculata*.

country, but the lesser short-tailed bat lives on islands and in certain areas of North Island native forest. There was also the greater short-tailed bat, however it succumbed more quickly to predators (kiore, laughing owls, rats, stoats and cats) and hasn't been seen since the late 1960s; it is now thought to be extinct.

Native bats are small enough to nestle in your hand. They are nocturnal, roost in hollow trees and caves and use high-pitched calls, or echolocation, to find their way about. The tiny lesser short-tailed bat is unusual for hunting on the ground, folding its wings to use like extra legs. In 2021, the long-tailed bat got extra publicity for winning the Bird of the Year competition.

NOT A CATERPILLAR, NOT A WORM

The peripatus/ngāokeoke (velvet worm), lives in rotting logs and under leaf litter on the forest floor. They are 2–8 cm long with 13–16 pairs of legs, slow moving and nocturnal; they look like caterpillars ('ngaoki' means 'to crawl'), but don't turn into moths or butterflies; they are not worms (despite their name) or insects, but something in-between. Their feeding methods are also unique: they fire a jet of sticky liquid to trap their prey and then inject them with saliva to dissolve and suck out the flesh inside.

Peripatus have changed very little over hundreds of millions of years. One population lives in the Caversham Valley Forest Reserve in south Dunedin, including in nearby gardens. When State Highway One at Caversham was widened in 2012, the New Zealand Transport Agency, Dunedin City Council, local residents, the Department of Conservation and others worked together to move and protect peripatus that would otherwise lose their habitat.

Velvet worm, *Onychophora*.

Another population was discovered in 2006 at Wimbledon, near Dannevirke. Twelve-year-old Kahn Coleman was working with farmer Brian Hales on a project to have a patch of bush on Hales' farm protected with a QEII covenant. Local rumour said that peripatus might live there; they searched for them and found some.

TUATARA

Tuatara belong to a group of reptiles called rhynchocephalia, which lived between 250 to 65 million years ago, alongside the dinosaurs. They are popularly known as 'living fossils', which implies they have hardly changed in millions of years. In fact, they have evolved and adapted over that time — but they are still remarkable and unique as the only surviving descendants of the rhynchocephalia.

To Māori, tuatara symbolise wisdom and a link to the spiritual world, and they are viewed as kaitiaki of special sites. The name means 'spines on the back' in te reo Māori, referring to the crest of spines that runs down the back and tail.

In the late 1800s and early 1900s, tuatara could still be found on the mainland. In 1896, a young man who had been to the North Island brought back a tuatara that he gave to the Invercargill Athenaeum, a public library and museum. The tuatara, named Joe, measured two feet (60 cm) 'from snout to tail'. He lived in a box and didn't eat for the first few months, apart from the odd fly, but a visitor suggested that he might eat live grubs dug out of rotten wood. Each morning after that the cleaner carefully brushed and fed him. He roamed the library shelves and knew his way around the building, upstairs and downstairs.

Joe died in July 1899, of old age or from a spell of frosty weather, but he enjoyed more freedom than tuatara kept in a glass case at the Colonial Museum in Wellington. One of them, thought to be over 100 years old, died in 1909 after 25 years in captivity. Māori would not go in to visit these captive tuatara and would rush away if they happened to catch sight of them.

A tuatara caught in Wadestown, a suburb of Wellington, was taken by a traveller by ship to be donated to Glasgow Zoo. Other tuatara

ABOVE Henry, the world's oldest tuatara in captivity. In early 2025 he was estimated to be over 120 years old.

TOP The preserved skull of a tuatara.

and native birds were sent to zoos and museums in Sydney, Vienna, London and New York.

In the early years of the twentieth century, some lighthouse keepers were given special payments for their work protecting tuatara (which are often called lizards, although they are not). They counted tuatara numbers, looked out for nests and tried to get rid of wild cats, hawks and goats, their predators. Some had tuatara living in their gardens. A keeper at Stephens Island in 1913 said, 'The lizards are very fond of wallowing in the pools of water after rain, and one that used to frequent a hole alongside my house would have his bath daily by means of a pan of water put there for him.'

Tuatara now live mostly on offshore islands, with an estimated 30,000–50,000 on Stephens Island/Takapourewa. The tuatarium at the Southland Museum and Art Gallery, Invercargill, also houses over a hundred of them. The oldest tuatara in captivity, named Henry by staff, has lived there for over 45 years. He became a father for the first time, aged over 100, to 11 hatchlings, in 2009.

RIGHT 'Tuātara' is a Māori word and means 'spines on the back'.

WĒTĀ

Fossil evidence shows that the ancestors of wētā have also been around since the age of the dinosaurs. They evolved into over 100 different species of giant, tusked, tree, ground and cave wētā, found everywhere from high mountains to hollow trees, sand dunes, soil burrows, under rocks, in dark caves and old mines, and in gardens, letterboxes and even gumboots.

The largest of the giant wētā is the wētāpunga, which now lives mostly on Little Barrier Island/ Hauturu-o-Toi and can weigh as much as a sparrow or mouse. The mountain stone wētā lives up to 1100 to 1500 metres above sea level, where it shelters under rock slabs and survives cold winters by freezing solid and thawing out in warmer weather.

Wētā can't fly but can jump with their strong back legs; the cave or jumping wētā can cover two metres in one leap. Aola Richards studied cave wētā in the 1950s, working by torchlight for seven weeks in the Waitomo Caves. To tell the wētā apart, she painted several hundred

Aola Richards with a cave wētā.

LEFT Cook Strait giant wētā, *Deinacrida rugosa.*

RIGHT Auckland tree wētā, *Hemideina thoracica.*

with coloured spots. Richards worked mostly on her own in the dark, away from the tourist routes, with occasional visits from the guides. 'Girl Braves Depths Of Caves To Study Wetas' was a typical newspaper headline. She didn't find it creepy being alone, but didn't like the furry black jumping spiders and always carried a stick to ward off the water rats, 'as big as small cats ... there are things in the caves the tourists have no idea of'. (*Press*, 14 July 1955) A species of cave wētā, *Miotopus richardsae,* was later named after her.

MOA

The last moa vanished generations ago, but these astonishing giant birds that were unique to this country still capture people's imaginations and appear in rock drawings, books, poems, paintings and reconstructions in museums.

The moa was a ratite (like the kiwi, emu and ostrich). There were nine different species, varying in size from the tallest birds ever, like the two-metre-tall South Island giant moa, to the turkey-sized little bush moa. They were all flightless, with no trace of wings, although recent research (based on genetic similarity to the South American tinamou, which can fly) suggests their ancestors flew here and gradually evolved to be flightless because they had no large predators (apart from the Haast's eagle) that they needed to escape from.

Moa lived across mainland New Zealand and offshore islands, in the mountains, grasslands, forests and along the coast. The first Polynesian arrivals easily stalked them or caught them in nooses and traps to provide plentiful food, feathers and skin. We know this because of bones found in middens (old rubbish heaps) and made into ornaments, fishhooks and other tools.

But moa were slow to reproduce — they only laid one or two eggs in a season and young moa took a long time to grow to mature birds, so they couldn't quickly replace the birds that were killed. Hunting and loss of habitat as forests were cleared meant they were probably extinct within a few hundred years of the first human arrivals, leaving evidence of their existence in bones, footprints, fragments of eggshells, and Māori memories and whakataukī, passed down in their oral traditions or written down by early European visitors.

Skeleton of upland moa, *Megalapteryx didinus*.

South Island giant moa *Dinornis robustus.*

Long lost bird 'seen by hikers'

By Our Auckland Correspondent

THREE hikers in New Zealand's high country claim to have seen a moa, a large, flightless bird believed to have become extinct nearly 500 years ago.

The hikers say they chased the bird in remote South Island bushland, 50 miles west of Christchurch, last Wednesday.

Mr Paddy Freaney, who owns a hotel in the area where he says he has seen and photographed the bird, said it had a thin, 3ft long neck and a small head and beak; its body, covered in reddy-brown and grey feathers, was about three feet above the ground.

Mr Andy Grant, an officer with the Department of Protected Species, said it was possible that the bird was an emu, which is bred on farms in the area. Local farmers say, however, that none of their emus is missing.

Mr Sam Waby, head of a school art department, and Miss Rochelle Rafferty, a gardener at Mr Freaney's hotel, said they saw the bird independently and at the same time as Mr Freaney.

Wildlife experts are examining the photographs and a search is being organised. "We are looking for feathers, droppings and any other clues," said Mr Grant.

Scientists, who have examined moa bones, believe they were hunted to extinction 500 years ago by Maoris, who arrived in New Zealand from Polynesia 1,000 years ago.

Ms Beverly McCulloch, a moa expert at Canterbury Museum, doubted the claims. She said: "The weight of scientific evidence is against it. The history of moa studies is littered with possible sightings, none of which has ever been proven, some of which were hoaxes and most which were wishful thinking.

"That does not preclude someone sighting a live moa. Nobody would be happier than me for that to happen."

The moa: thought to have been hunted to extinction

Newspaper article about Paddy Freaney's moa sighting.

John Harris, a trader living in Poverty Bay, sailed to Sydney in 1837 and left a collection of items for his uncle, Dr John Rule. It included a small piece of bone found in a riverbed which Māori told Harris came from an eagle-like bird, now extinct. Back in England, Rule showed the bone to Professor Richard Owen.

Owen deduced from the bone fragment that the moa was a new species of large flightless bird. He called it 'an unknown struthious bird of large size, presumed to be extinct' and named it *Dinornis novaezealandiae*, meaning giant, surprising or prodigious bird from New Zealand. ('Struthious' means like an ostrich or similar bird. Owen also named the dinosaur, using fossil evidence to deduce a newly discovered order of animals, which he called Dinosauria.) The moa bone is now in the Natural History Museum in London.

Richard Owen.

Preserved moa feathers.

William Colenso said no Māori had ever seen a moa, so he believed they must be extinct or Māori would have found them, but stories of possible sightings lingered for years.

Alice McKenzie grew up in Martins Bay and remembered, aged seven, getting close enough to stroke a huge bird before it chased her. This was in 1880 and she said that footprints were seen each year there until 1907. Geoffrey Orbell, who rediscovered the takahē, thought moa might have survived in Fiordland until the early nineteenth century. As late as 1950, the *Otago Daily Times* reported that moa might be alive in remote parts of the Murchison Range. In 1993, Paddy Freaney, who ran a pub near Arthur's Pass, was sure he'd seen a moa in the bush and took a fuzzy photo of it.

WHO NAMES THE ANIMALS?

The first Polynesian arrivals gave names to the birds and animals they found, often based on their distinctive call, such as kea, kiwi or kākā. 'Ruru' sounded like that to Māori, although Europeans later heard its cry as 'more pork'. The word moa may come from a Polynesian term for domestic fowl. Other names, such as kōtare (kingfisher) and kōtuku (white heron) are the same as in other Pasifika countries. Birds can have more than one Māori name, given by different iwi or to reflect different life stages.

Scientific names can be quirky. Six species of native wasp were named after characters from *The Hobbit* by J.R.R. Tolkien (*Shireplitis bilboi* was named after Bilbo Baggins). The Gravel maggot, *Smeagol climoi*, was named for another Tolkien character.

Many animals and birds have been named after people. Buller's albatross, *Thalassarche bulleri*, and Buller's shearwater, *Ardenna bulleri*, were named after Walter Buller. Haast's eagle was named after Julius von Haast, who found its bones in swampland on a South Island station owned by George Moore; its scientific name is *Hieraaetus moorei*. Archey's frog was named after Gilbert Edward Archey, director of the Auckland Museum. The South Island takahē was named *Porphyrio hochstetteri* after Austrian geologist Ferdinand von Hochstetter.

Sir Walter Buller, c. 1903.

Some names can now seem to display historic and cultural bias, reflecting colonial history. They ignore indigenous names and don't describe anything about the species itself.

Today, local iwi and hapū might be involved in choosing a name for a newly discovered species. Iwi from Great Barrier Island/Aotea gave the chevron skink the name niho taniwha, or teeth of the taniwha, because of the V-shaped markings on its back. Te mokomoko a Tohu, New Zealand's second largest gecko found on The Brothers/ Ngāwhatu-Kai-ponu in Cook Strait, was gifted its name by Te Ātiawa o Te Waka-a-Māui in honour of Tohu Kākahi, Parihaka leader and pacifist, who would have passed the islands on his way to prison in Dunedin.

Taxonomy

Taxonomy is the branch of science devoted to describing and classifying new species. Scientific names are often derived from Greek or Latin words and follow the Linnaean system for classifying living things, developed by Swedish naturalist Carl Linnaeus. They are written in italics and in two parts. The first part, with a capital letter, shows the genus. The second, without a capital letter, identifies the species within the genus. The scientific name of a species is usually given by the person who formally identifies it.

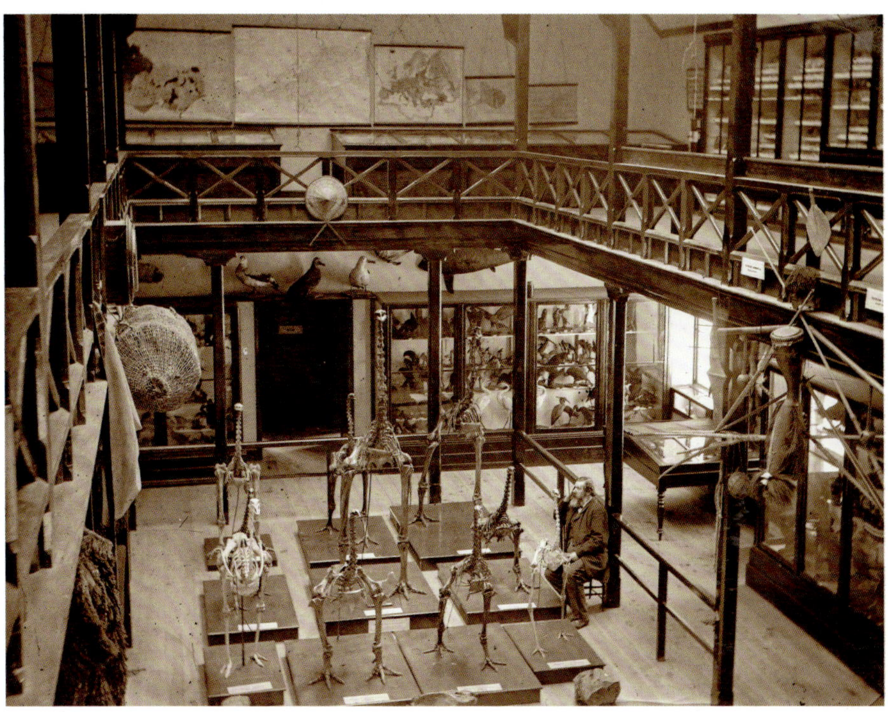

Canterbury Museum founder Julius von Haast in the Mountfort Gallery, c. 1872.

THE FIRST PEOPLE

POLYNESIAN ARRIVALS

The first Polynesian arrivals brought kūmara and two mammals: the kurī (dog) and kiore (Polynesian rat). Finding food in a new land was crucial. Over several hundred years, moa and other bird species were hunted to extinction and the numbers of marine mammals (like seals) plummeted. Fish, shellfish, eels/tuna and plants would have provided food instead.

Māori have a special relationship with the land and its native animals and plants. The legends of Kupe and Māui are intertwined

Sydney Parkinson accompanied explorer James Cook on his first voyage to New Zealand. In this scene he depicts a white dog sitting near the rear of the waka.

Polynesian rat, *Rattus exulans*, Māori name: kiore.

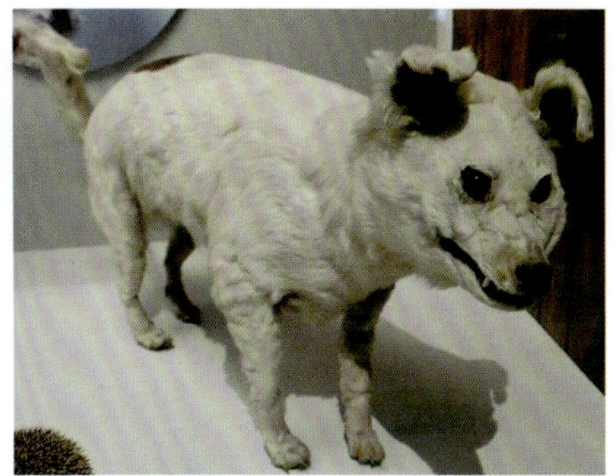

Kūri, *Canis lupus familiaris*. This specimen was collected in 1876 and is at Te Papa Tongarewa, Wellington.

with sea creatures (Kupe chasing the octopus/wheke, Māui hauling up the giant fish). There are many pūrākau or Māori legends about the creatures that live here. All native species are highly valued and some have particular cultural significance. Te raukura, the white feathers of the albatross/toroa, were worn by Te Whiti o Rongomai, Tohu Kākahi and their followers as a symbol of Parihaka's passive resistance movement and continues today as a symbol of harmony, unity, hope and peace.

EARLY EUROPEAN EXPLORERS

The first European explorers sailed with animals on board for food and companionship. Cats prowled around the ships, hunting for rats. Joseph Banks often took his two dogs ashore with him. Poultry, sheep, cattle and pigs lived in cages and pens on upper decks, exposed to the weather and fierce waves. Birds that flew into the cabins were kept as pets. Other animals were picked up at stops on the way and used for trade or barter.

Lieutenant (later Captain) James Cook sailed on three separate expeditions to New Zealand. Each voyage took years, so he was always looking for fresh food to ward off scurvy. On his first visit on the *Endeavour* he found kurī but no other animals, so on his second and third voyages he intentionally released plants and animals including hens, goats, sheep and pigs, some as gifts to Māori but others as sources of food for future expeditions.

These animals had mixed survival rates. The first that Cook released were geese in Dusky Sound, never seen again. A pair of sheep were found dead. Cook wrote on 23 May 1773,

> Last Night the Ewe and Ram I had with so much care and trouble brought to this place, died, we did suppose that they were poisoned by eating of some poisonous plant, thus all my fine hopes of stocking this Country with a breed of Sheep were blasted in a moment.

CREATURES OF RIVERS AND SEA

In May 1773, Cook noted in his journal that Dusky Sound abounded with fish, shellfish and seals 'in great numbers'. Shiploads of sealers and whalers soon arrived, braving harsh weather conditions and a tough working life for whale oil, baleen, ambergris and seal skins.

Whales were slaughtered around New Zealand and throughout the Pacific. The Southern right whale/tohorā, once common offshore, was almost wiped out. By the 1920s, there were as few as 40 left in New Zealand waters. After that, none were seen for decades, until reports began to trickle out of sightings near the Auckland Islands and Campbell Islands. This was confirmed by air force pilots who flew over the islands in 1992 and spotted dozens of whales. Tohorā numbers have slowly recovered to about 2000 around the coast today.

Body of a humpback whale being processed at the Perano Whaling Station, 1948.

Longfin eel, *Anguilla dieffenbachii.*

The last whale killed by New Zealand whalers was a sperm whale, harpooned off Kaikoura on 21 December 1964 by men from the Perano Whaling Station in Tory Channel. Today, Kaikoura and Cook Strait/Raukawa lie on the path of migrating humpback whales on their 5000 km journey from the cold Antarctic waters of the Southern Ocean to the warmer Pacific Ocean, where they breed and have their calves.

New Zealand longfin eels/tuna also carry out astonishing migrations, hatching into larvae in the Pacific Ocean and reaching New Zealand on ocean currents, swimming upriver as juvenile or glass eels, living in rivers and streams as elvers and adult eels, and finally, when they might be up to a hundred years old, setting off back to the Pacific. Nobody knows exactly where they lay their eggs, but it is somewhere near Tonga, thousands of kilometres from here.

NATIVE ANIMALS

Walter Buller, born to missionary parents in Hokianga, was a magistrate, interpreter, lawyer, te reo speaker and ornithologist. *A history of the birds of New Zealand* (published in five parts between 1872–73) contained descriptions of 147 species. It was a big, expensive book with colour paintings by Johannes Keulemans, a Dutch artist who never came to New Zealand.

Huia, *Heteralocha acutirostris*, by Johannes Keulemans, 1888.

Buller was also a bird collector. He thought that native birds were bound to go extinct and he wanted to find specimens before they disappeared. In his 1892 paper 'Further Notes on the Birds of New Zealand', Buller described heading into the bush at the back of Waikanae and only seeing one huia, where five or six years earlier they would have been plentiful. But that didn't stop him from killing them to add to his collections. This was his account of an expedition into the Wairarapa in 1883:

> In a few seconds, without sound or warning of any kind, a Huia came bounding along, almost tumbling, through the close foliage of the pukapuka, and presented himself to view at such close range that it was impossible to fire. This gave me an opportunity of watching this beautiful bird and marking his noble bearing, if I may so express it, before I shot him.

Later that day, the hunters stopped to watch two kererū.

> Whilst we were looking at and admiring this little picture of bird-life, a pair of Huias, without uttering a sound, appeared in a tree overhead, and as they were caressing each other with their beautiful bills, a charge of No. 6 brought both to the ground together. The incident was rather touching, and I felt almost glad that the shot was not mine, although by no means loth to appropriate the two fine specimens.

This was the age of the collector, hunting down specimens for museums and collections around the world. Andreas Reischek came to New Zealand from 1877 to 1889, leaving his new wife behind in Austria. He was a taxidermist at Canterbury Museum, but also travelled around the country and outer islands, building up a huge collection of birds, lizards and other specimens, including stitchbirds/hihi on visits to Little Barrier Island/Te Hauturu-o-Toi where they were already rare.

Reischek warned of the dangers of stoats and ferrets, and wanted Little Barrier Island to be made a nature reserve, but like other collectors he shot and killed birds to obtain specimens for

Kākāpō specimens at the Natural History Museum in Vienna.

museums in case they were lost forever. The Natural History Museum in Vienna contains over 400 birds that he collected.

LOST, FOUND, OVERLOOKED AND ENDANGERED

On 17 January 1770, Joseph Banks marvelled at the sound of the dawn chorus in Queen Charlotte Sound. 'Their voices were certainly the most melodious wild musick I have ever heard, almost imitating small bells but with the most tuneable silver sound imaginable.'

Today, as Sir Paul Callaghan said in 2012, 'our forests have never been so silent'. He estimated there were 70 million possums, and counting rodents, mustelids and cats as well, maybe 300 million pests targeting native species. The Department of Conservation National Predator Control Programme annual report for 2024 estimated that 25 million native birds are killed every year by rats, stoats, possums and other predators.

From 1861 onwards, Parliament passed a series of Acts to protect birds and animals, but these were often to protect them outside the game or hunting season, so there would be good numbers when the season opened. For many years it was legal to shoot native birds during the game season. Robert Gillies, an Otago MP, wrote in 1877 that 'it used to be a common recipe amongst early settlers, that it took fourteen pigeons and one kaka parrot to make good soup.' Birds could only be protected by listing them as 'native game' and then making them exempt from hunting, as happened first with the tūī in 1878.

The Animals Protection Acts of 1907 and 1910 listed native species that were given full protection, including birds and tuatara (and, in 1907, the possum, even though not a native). Still in force is the Wildlife Act 1953 and its amendments, under which most native birds, frogs, bats, lizards and tuatara are protected.

But legal protection came too late for many. Extinct birds include the 11 species of moa, Haast's eagle, adzebill, New Zealand quail, Chatham Island fernbird, North Island snipe, New Zealand bittern, Lyall's wren, North Island and South Island piopio, laughing owl/whēkau, huia and the South Island snipe.

North Island adzebill, *Aptornis otidiformis*.

South Island adzebill, *Aptornis defossor*.

The New Zealand Threat Classification System (NZTCS) uses expert advice to fit native animals, plants and fungi into categories and assess the risk of extinction. The category of Resident is broken down into Extinct, Threatened, At Risk and Not Threatened, with extra levels under Threatened and At Risk, and another category for Insufficient Data, if there isn't much information available. There is a separate category for Introduced and Naturalised.

The category of Non-resident includes migratory birds. Coastal habitats at Miranda, Muriwai, Foxton Beach, Farewell Spit and Cape Kidnappers make temporary homes for migratory shore birds like godwits, terns, curlews, dotterels, plovers and sandpipers. Two land birds (the shining cuckoo and long-tailed cuckoo) also migrate each year.

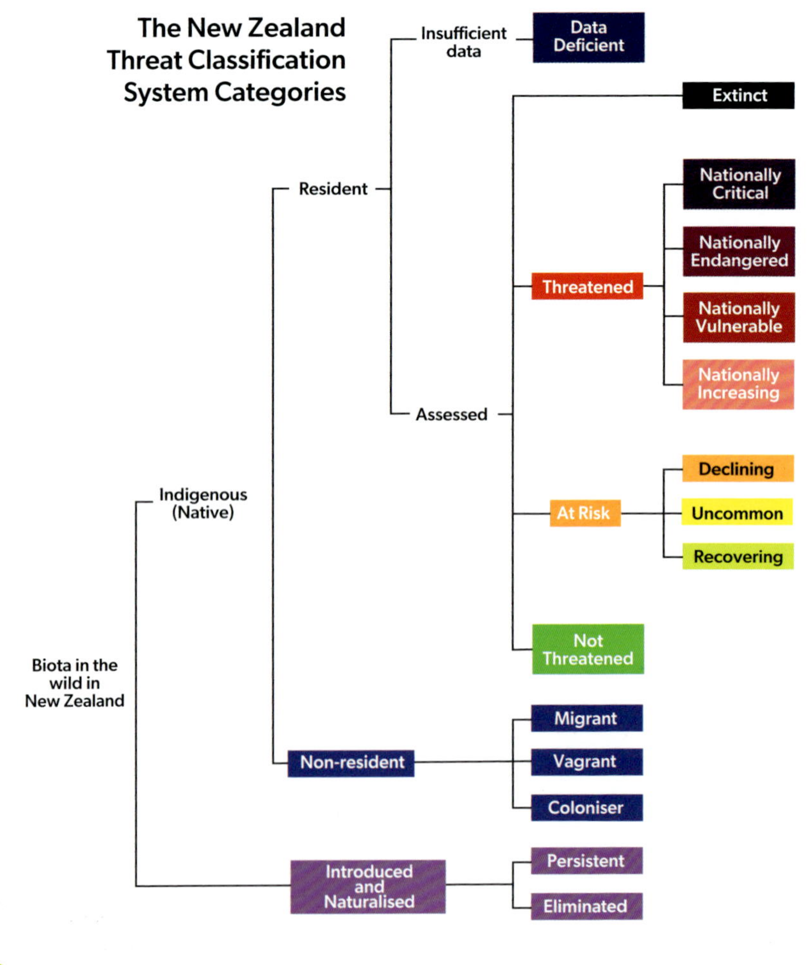

VANISHED: GONE FOREVER

HUIA

The huia was renowned for its haunting call and was unusual because male and female had different beak shapes. Its feathers were a mark of status for Māori; only chiefs were allowed to wear the white-tipped tail feathers.

William Onslow was governor from 1889 to 1892, and his second son was the first vice-regal baby born in New Zealand. Ngāti Huia, a hapū of Ngāti Raukawa, gifted the baby a Māori name and he was christened Victor Alexander Herbert Huia Onslow at St Paul's, Wellington, on 26 January 1891. The mayor put a huia feather into his headdress. Later that year, baby Huia was presented to Ngāti Huia at a ceremony at Raukawa marae in Ōtaki and a kaumātua (elder) asked Governor Onslow to protect the huia, which were being killed to meet overseas demand for exotic specimens.

Rewi Manga Maniapoto (Ngāti Maniapoto), 1879, with huia feathers. Maniapoto, a chief, was renowned for being a skilled military tactician and leader, especially during the Waikato War.

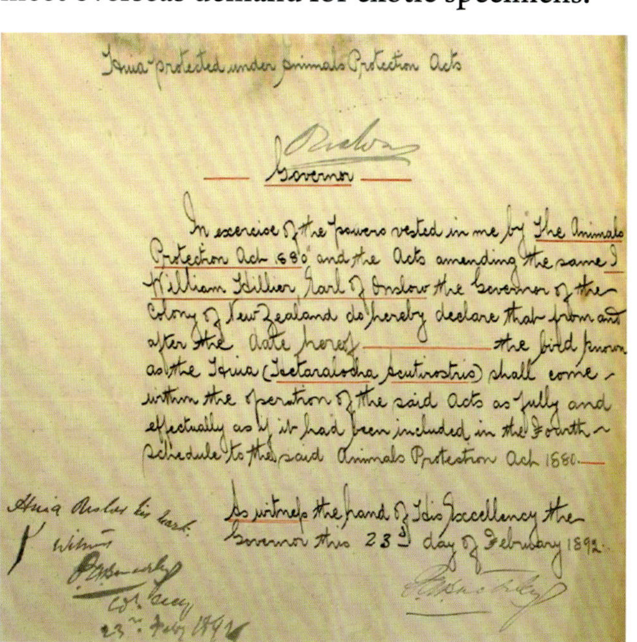

Huia protected under Animals Protection Acts

Onslow

Governor

In exercise of the powers vested in me by The Animals Protection Act 1880 and the Acts amending the same I William Hillier Earl of Onslow the Governor of the Colony of New Zealand do hereby declare that from and after the date hereof the bird known as the Huia (Heteralocha acutirostris) shall come within the operation of the said Acts as fully and effectually as if it had been included in the Fourth Schedule to the said Animals Protection Act 1880.

As witness the hand of His Excellency the Governor this 23rd day of February 1892.

Huia Onslow his mark.
witness
Col. Secy
23rd Feby 1892

The warrant to protect huia signed by Governor Onslow on 23 February 1892. The mark at lower left was made by Huia Onslow, aged 15 months.

Governor Onslow wrote a paper on Native New Zealand Birds and asked Parliament to 'throw over this bird the shield of government protection'. When he signed the warrant to protect the huia, 15-month-old Huia Onslow added his scribbled mark under his father's signature.

The last official huia sighting was of two males and a female on 28 December 1907.

The Duke and Duchess of York, later King George V and Queen Mary, visited New Zealand in 1901 and again in 1927. In Rotorua, Māori presented them with gifts of huia feathers put into his hatband and her hat. This was a mark of respect, but it sparked a fashion for the feathers that European hatmakers rushed to imitate.

On 6 December 2022, Charles Royal presented a submission to the Waitangi Tribunal on behalf of Ngāti Kikopiri, a hapū of Ngāti Raukawa and Ngāti Huia. He spoke of the significance of the huia and its loss.

> We can no longer hear our ancestor calling in the forest or sing about the loyalty of huia couples while witnessing that loyalty

Duke and Duchess of York with huia feathers in their hats after a reception, 1927.

> express itself before us. The loss of mana and the loss of identity experienced by our people of Ngāti Kikopiri at the hands of Crown and its agents is poignantly and sadly symbolised by the loss of the huia.

In 2024, a huia feather expected to attract bids of a few thousand dollars sold in Auckland for NZ$46,521— a world record for a single feather.

LAST SIGHTINGS

Haast's eagle, with its 2–3-metre wingspan and powerful talons, was strong enough to attack and kill moa. We know this because moa bones have been found with puncture marks that nothing except this huge bird could have made. Recorded in early Māori rock art paintings, the Haast's eagle may also represent the giant bird or pouākai of Māori legend, but it didn't survive after much of its habitat was lost to deforestation by fire and its main prey, the moa, was hunted to extinction.

Charles Douglas and his dog, Betsey Jane, c. 1894.

Charles Douglas, or 'Mr Explorer Douglas', was a Scottish surveyor who explored and mapped Westland's mountains, rivers, valleys and glaciers for over forty years, often with only a dog for company. 'I never kill bird or beast for sport, and hate to see anyone doing it,' he said. But he travelled light through rough country and depended on the bush for food, so he often killed birds to eat.

About the harrier hawk/kāhu, he wrote, 'The expanse of wing of this bird will scarcely be believed. One was eight foot four inches from tip to tip, the other was six feet nine inches.' It's possible that these giant birds, nesting on crags, were not hawks at all, but some of the last surviving Haast's eagles. However Douglas shot them, so there is no proof of what he saw.

EXTINCT OR NOT? KŌKAKO

The elusive South Island kōkako/kōkā, called the 'grey ghost', has been heard but never photographed or captured. It was declared extinct in 2007, then reclassified as data deficient in 2013 after an accepted sighting near Reefton, but some backcountry users and deer hunters believe they have seen it since or heard its unique bell-like song. The South Island Kōkako Charitable Trust's website has an interactive map logging possible kōkako encounters, and a $10,000 reward is on offer for information that proves the bird still exists.

North Island kōkako, *Callaeas wilsoni*.

South Island kōkako, *Callaeas cinereus*.

In contrast, the number of breeding pairs of the North Island kōkako (the bird on the New Zealand $50 note, known for the way it hops and runs along or glides between branches) has increased from 330 in the late 1990s to 2000 pairs today. In 1978, conservation protesters occupied Pureora Forest Park, perching on platforms in the trees and sitting on logs, to stop logging of native tōtara where the kōkako lived.

SUCCESS STORIES: SAVED

BLACK ROBIN/KAKARUIA

By 1977, there were seven black robins left on Little Mangere Island/Tapuaenuku in the Chatham Archipelago, and only one breeding female, given the name Old Blue.

Don Merton led a team to move the birds to a nearby, bigger home. They caught them with nets, put them in boxes, carried them down the cliffs and rowed across to Mangere Island. For five years, until she died at 14, Old Blue laid one or two clutches of eggs each season. The rescue team removed some eggs to encourage her to lay more, and put them into the nests of Chathams tomtits to hatch. Thanks to Old Blue, by 2021 there were about 300 black robins left.

Black robin, *Petroica traversi*.

Kunekune, *Sus scrofa domesticus*. In Māori 'kunekune' means fat and round.

KUNEKUNE

Kunekune are placid, quiet and gentle. They are smaller than other pigs, with short legs and bellies low to the ground, and have piri piri, or wattles, hanging from their jaws. Their hair can be short, long, straight or curly, and their coats can be one colour (like brown, tan, black, white or gold) or a mix in spots and splodges.

The origins of kunekune are unclear but DNA testing shows that they share characteristics with pigs in Asia, South America and Polynesia. The Vietnamese pot-bellied pig, for example, is another small friendly pig with short legs, named after its low-slung belly, which can almost touch the ground.

There are many ways that kunekune might have got here. Traders brought Chinese pigs to England from the 1700s on. These small, black pigs interbred with the bigger English pigs to

BELOW Staglands founder John Simister, along with Michael Willis, is credited with saving the kunekune from extinction in the 1970s.

produce a breed that was rounder and fattened quicker. Other small domestic pigs from China or Southeast Asia might have spread with long-distance journeys across the Pacific (and from there to New Zealand), or through trading with whalers. The Poland China pig, first bred in Ohio, USA in the mid-1800s, is one of the few other pigs to have hanging wattles and could have arrived here with American whalers, but it's a big pig (and despite the name does not trace its ancestry back to China).

Māori looked after kunekune and treated them as pets, food sources and items for barter, trade or gifting. But by the 1970s, there weren't many pure-bred kunekune left. They could easily have died out as a breed if not for the efforts of two men and the help they were given by Māori families and farmers.

John Simister and Michael Willis both owned wildlife parks: Staglands Wildlife Reserve, north of Wellington, and Willowbank Wildlife Reserve in Christchurch. Looking for kunekune, they slung a crate in the back of a ute and set off on a search to remote and isolated areas of the North Island.

They talked with Māori who valued kunekune as part of their traditional culture. Many people hadn't seen kunekune for years but they directed them to farmhouses and communities deep in the bush. Simister and Willis collected about 18 kunekune and used them as the basis of two different breeding groups, to start building up the population again.

DISCOVERIES: LOST AND FOUND

Many native species have vanished, however there are also stories of species newly discovered, saved, or rediscovered when everyone thought they had been — or were about to be — lost.

TĀIKO

The Westland black petrel/tāiko was discovered after museum director Robert Falla gave a radio talk about muttonbirding in 1945. He mentioned that muttonbirds/tītī bred in summer. Children at remote Barrytown School on the West Coast wrote to tell him

Black petrel/tāiko, *Procellaria parkinsoni.*

about a colony of muttonbirds nearby that bred in winter. Falla came to inspect the birds and found they weren't, in fact, muttonbirds, and he announced the discovery of a new black petrel.

Takahē, *Porphyrio hochstetteri.*

TAKAHĒ

The takahē is a large flightless bird, related to (but bigger than) the pūkeko. Sealers' dogs caught one on Resolution Island and a few other specimens were collected, but after the 1890s there were no proven sightings for fifty years.

Geoffrey Orbell, an Invercargill doctor, was convinced that takahē might still exist in remote parts of Fiordland. On a deer hunting trip to the Murchison Mountains, he heard an unfamiliar bird call and saw tracks. He led a group back to the area in November 1948. 'I knew from the evidence the birds were there. They had to be there, and we set out to prove it,' he said.

LEFT AND RIGHT Takahē have remarkable blue/green iridescent feathers and a sturdy red beak.

They got up early and climbed for three and a half hours to a clearing where a bird suddenly appeared out of the snowgrass. Crouching down, Orbell took a photo while the three others crept up and threw a net over it. They caught and photographed two live takahē (and saw another one) before letting them go.

Elwyn Welch farmed near Mt Bruce in the Wairarapa. Known for his skills in hand-raising endangered birds, he was chosen to be part of a programme to breed takahē in captivity. In preparation, he trained his bantam hens to stay sitting on boiled eggs in wooden boxes, even when he carried them in his backpack or drove them on his tractor around his farm. He added pūkeko eggs to their nests to make sure they would raise other chicks. In 1957, and again in 1959, he set off — with the hens — on the long journey to Fiordland, and returned with takahē chicks safely nestled under the foster bantam hens. Captive breeding did not prove easy, but the first takahē chicks were hatched at Mt Bruce in 1972.

In 1961, Welch and his family went to Nigeria where he and his wife Shirley worked as missionaries, but he caught polio and died, aged only 36. Their farm near Masterton was the foundation for what is now Pūkaha National Wildlife Centre at Mt Bruce.

The Burwood Takahē Centre near Te Anau opened in 1985. Department of Conservation rangers used takahē hand puppets to make sure the chicks did not get too used to humans. The birds now raise their own chicks within a safe enclosure. In 2023, there were about 500 takahē left. They live in wildlife centres, on predator-free islands and in the wild in places such as the Murchison Mountains.

Other native creatures thought to have been lost and rediscovered (sometimes called a Lazarus species):

Campbell Island teal, *Anas nesiotis.*

- The Campbell Island teal, a small, flightless, mostly nocturnal duck, was presumed extinct after Norway rats overran its habitat on Campbell Island. In 1975, one was spotted on a nearby rat-free rocky islet called Dent Island. A small population was taken to Pūkaha National Wildlife Centre to be part of a captive breeding programme and one of them, Daisy, raised 24 ducklings over 12 years, helping to save the species.

Frosted phoenix, *Titanomis sisyrota,* drawn by George Vernon Hudson in 1928.

- The frosted phoenix, a large moth, had only ten recorded sightings (two by women at home) between the 1870s and 1959, until a Swedish tourist on a birdwatching visit to Stewart Island/Rakiura took a photo of one fluttering around a light outside his hotel in March 2024.

Canterbury knobbled weevil, *Hadramphus tuberculatus.*

- The Canterbury knobbled weevil, a flightless beetle covered in bumpy nodules that lives among the spiky leaves of speargrass plants, was presumed extinct after last being seen in

1922. But in 2004, a biology student working in the Burkes Pass Scenic Reserve found a colony in a patch of land near the main road, where they are now protected by a fence from rabbits and hedgehogs. In 2024, a farmer checking a trapline came across a new population of them at Ashburton Lakes/Ōtūwharekai.

ENDANGERED: STILL AT RISK

KĀKĀPŌ

The kākāpō is flightless, nocturnal and the world's largest parrot, known for its male courtship routine of building bowl systems connected by tracks and booming through the night to attract a female. Charlie Douglas wrote that 'the birds used to be in dozens round the camp, screeching and yelling ... and at times it was impossible to sleep for the noise'. But by the 1890s, its habitat had shrunk to remote mountain valleys of Fiordland.

Resolution Island in Dusky Sound, Fiordland, was New Zealand's first wildlife reserve, and Richard Henry was its first caretaker. He lived there from 1894 to 1908, finding kiwi and kākāpō in the bush on the mainland with the help of a muzzled dog, and moving them in cages by boat to the island. He moved 700 birds in this way, often on his own and in the face of wild and stormy weather, and sent others to museums, gardens and reserves.

Sirocco the kākāpō, *Strigops habroptilus*, Maud Island.

LEFT Lassie, Richard Henry's dog.
RIGHT Richard Henry.

Henry thought the birds would be safe on the island, not realising that the channel between it and the mainland was narrow enough for predators to swim across. In August 1901, he was alarmed to spot a weasel: 'quite a little thing, no bigger than a rat, and nearly white in colour ... I have been out with the gun every fine day since ... but have not seen it again.'

He was heartbroken when he found a stoat on the island in 1904, realising the birds he had tried to protect were doomed, but he holds a special place in the history of the kākāpō and conservation. In 1908 he was appointed the first caretaker of Kāpiti Island, which had become a forest and bird reserve in 1897.

The name kākāpō comes from te reo Māori for parrot (kākā) and night (pō), and each individual kākāpō is also given its own name by the Kākāpō Recovery Group. Kākāpō numbers stayed low for years, but in 1974, 18 birds were found in Fiordland and transferred to safety on Maud Island/Te Hoiere. In 1977, a population of about 200 was found on Stewart Island, including (three years later) the first female to be found in 80 years. Today kākāpō live on predator-free offshore islands such as Codfish Island/Whenua Hou; some were also moved to Sanctuary Mountain Maungatautari in 2023. But threats to their existence continue and there are fewer than 250 alive.

KIWI

In 1811, Captain Andrew Barclay returned to England after a round-the-world voyage and presented the skin of a flightless bird to George Shaw, Zoology Keeper at the British Museum. The bird was probably found by sealers on Stewart Island/Rakiura and Shaw named it *Apteryx australis*. This holotype specimen — the one from which the species was named — is now held at World Museum Liverpool.

North Island brown kiwi, *Apteryx mantelli*.

To Māori, the kiwi is a very special bird, known as 'te manu huna a Tāne' or 'the hidden bird of Tāne', meaning it is protected by Tānemahuta, god of the forest.

It is also an iconic bird that has become a symbol for the nation and a nickname for its people. Soldiers still waiting to sail home carved the Bulford Kiwi into the chalky hillside of southern England in 1919. By the end of the First World War, and especially during the Second World War, New Zealand troops were known as 'kiwis'.

Kiwi (there are five different species) are flightless and nocturnal with strong, powerful legs, and feet with sharp claws. Their nostrils are at the end of their long beak and they have an excellent sense of smell. Their eggs are huge for their size, taking up about 20% of the female's body weight.

Like other native birds, they are at risk from predators and habitat loss, and even cars. Many chicks are killed by stoats; only one in twenty of those born in the wild survive to adulthood. Operation Nest Egg was launched in 1995 to find kiwi eggs and hatch them in safety, keeping the chicks in predator-proof sanctuaries until they are big enough to defend themselves. These birds have a much better chance of survival when returned to their habitats.

THE SMALL AND OVERLOOKED

Some native insects, like the glow-worm, red admiral butterfly and cicada, are well known. But most insects and invertebrates (animals without a backbone) like spiders, worms, snails and slugs don't win the same attention as native birds. They are often small, camouflaged, nocturnal or crepuscular (come out at dawn and dusk), cryptic (hard to spot) and might only survive in remote habitats, however they play crucial roles in maintaining the bush ecosystem.

In New Zealand, there are more than 20,000 known species of insects, and about 18,000 are endemic. There are 6000 species of beetles, 2000 moths and butterflies, 2300 flies, 1100 spiders and 1000 land snails, along with 170 species of earthworms, 100 wētā and 85 millipedes.

George Hudson came to New Zealand as a boy with his family in 1881. For over 30 years he went looking for moths two or three nights every week in the bush-covered hills near his home in Karori, Wellington. His huge collection of specimens is now held at Te Papa Tongarewa.

New species are still being discovered. Scientists saw the New Zealand batfly for the first time when an ancient kauri known as Kopi in Northland collapsed in 1973. Kopi was home to a colony of short-tailed bats, and a Forest Service officer found small, blind, wingless flies clinging onto the bats' fur. He sent some dead specimens in a tin to Bev Holloway, an entomologist at the Department of Scientific and Industrial Research in Auckland. She discovered that the batfly relies on the short-tailed bat for transport and the warmth of the colony, and in return, it cleans up the roost by feeding on bat guano. She kept some batflies that couldn't be rehomed in a plastic box in her airing cupboard and fed them on mashed banana and yeast.

CLOCKWISE FROM TOP LEFT Some of New Zealand's smallest native and endemic creatures include the giant pill millipede, *Procyliosoma tuberculatum*, the leaf-veined slug, *Pseudaneitea papillata,* Sheetweb spider, genus Cambridgea and the New Zealand flatworm, *Arthurdendyus triangulatus*.

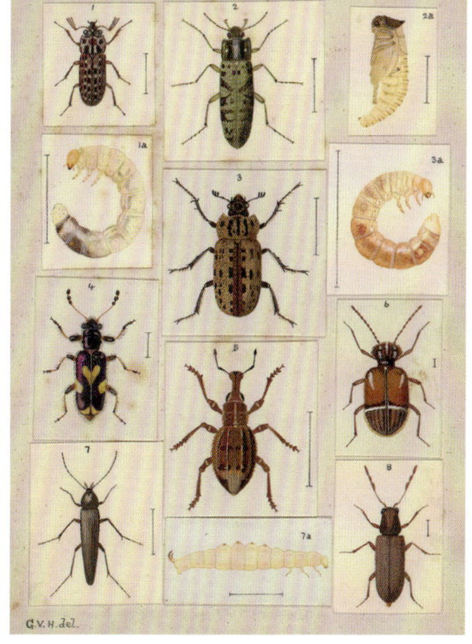

LEFT New Zealand batflies, *Mystacinobia zelandica*, on a juvenile short-tailed bat, *Mystacina turberculata*, in Fiordland.

RIGHT Hand-painted imagery of New Zealand beetles by George Hudson.

TOP Otago skink, *Oligosoma otagense*.

ABOVE Cobble skink, *Oligosoma aff. infrapanctatum 'cobble'*

LIZARDS/MOKOMOKO

Joan Robb wrote *New Zealand Amphibians and Reptiles* in 1980, listing about 36 known species of native lizards. Today there are 125: 77 skinks and 48 geckos. Many have been found by trampers, or by scientists or students searching for some other species.

Like all lizards, these geckos and skinks are ectotherms, meaning their body temperature is regulated by the environment around them. They are experts at using rocks and crannies to provide warmth or shade. All but one species give birth to live young, not eggs, which is unusual, but helps protect the baby lizards for longer.

Skinks have smaller eyes, a less obvious neck, pointy toes and firm skin covered with shiny scales. Geckos have bigger heads, bulging eyes, rounded toes and loose soft skin, and are good climbers. Both can have beautiful camouflage markings. They can be long-lived; two geckos marked in 1967 and 1969 by Tony Whitaker (who invented a method of finding lizards at night, using binoculars and a head torch to capture the glint of their eyes) were at least 64 and 60 years old when found again in 2025.

Lizards are at risk from predators such as birds, cats, weasels, rats, hedgehogs and tuatara, and from loss of habitat. Until 1981, they were not a protected species and could be caught and kept as pets. Today they are protected under the Wildlife Act. During roadworks for the Transmission Gully motorway north of Wellington, native lizards were moved to Ngā Manu Nature Reserve, Waikanae, for two years.

In April 2018, they were blessed by local kaumātua and released to a new habitat, a rock pile with spaces big enough to shelter in, but too small for mice to enter.

Moving lizards to new homes is a challenge because they have often adapted to very specific habitats: forest, tussock, shorelines, rocky outcrops or even alpine cliffs. Some have been taken to pest-free offshore islands, however they don't always adapt to the new environment.

The cobble skink was found in 2007, living in the gaps between beach cobble stones in a small area of coastline at Granity, near Westport. Coastal erosion, rising sea levels and storms threatened the area, and in 2016 Department of Conservation staff rescued about 30 of them and took them to Auckland Zoo. Later, Cyclone Gita blew through and destroyed their beach home and the skinks were thought to be extinct in the wild, but in 2021 Department of Conservation workers found more populations and in January 2025 the skinks from Auckland Zoo, including some bred in captivity, were returned to the West Coast.

North Island green gecko, *Naultinus grayii.*

The rarity and beauty of native lizards also puts them in danger. Poachers can sell them to overseas collectors for thousands of dollars. In 2010, a German tourist was fined and sentenced to 14 weeks in jail for trading in endangered species and hunting protected wildlife. He collected 44 geckos and skinks, including pregnant females, during a campervan trip around the South Island but was caught at Christchurch International Airport with them hidden in his clothes.

FROM TOP Hochstetter's frog, *Leiopelma hochstetteri;* Archey's frog, *Leiopelma archeyi;* Hamilton's frog, *Leiopelma hamiltoni.*

NATIVE FROGS/PEPEKETUA

New Zealand's native frogs — Archey's, Hochstetter's, Hamilton's and the closely-related Maud Island frog — are unique in many ways. They don't croak like other frogs, and their eggs hatch into live froglets, not tadpoles.

Maud Island frogs have been successfully transferred to other predator-free islands in the Marlborough Sounds, but Hamilton's frog lives mostly in one small area on Stephens Island/ Takapourewa where there may be only about 300 left. They were named after Harold Hamilton, a zoologist who collected a specimen from under a rock there in 1918; he later became the first director of the School of Māori Arts at Rotorua.

Other frog species were introduced from Australia. The Australian green frog or golden bell frog arrived here in the 1860s.

A story from the West Coast told how a local lawyer brought some Australian tree frogs, also known as whistling frogs, in a glass bottle from Tasmania in 1875 and emptied them into a drain in Greymouth.

GIANT SNAILS

New Zealand has many species of native land snails, including the enormous, nocturnal, carnivorous snails called Powelliphanta. The biggest ones weigh 90 g and they live up to 20 years.

Most Powelliphanta have small and localised habitats and don't travel far. *Powelliphanta augusta* is named for where it was found in 2005, on Mt Augustus on the West Coast, near the Stockton opencast coal mine. Mining was temporarily ceased with the mining industry and conservation groups at loggerheads over the future of the snails, but later the mining went ahead. Department of Conservation staff searched the area and collected over 6000 snails, with samples of vegetation and soil. They kept the snails in ice-cream containers on beds of moss in refrigerators and gradually released them to nearby sites, and ran a breeding programme while waiting to see if the snails would adapt to their new habitats. In 2011, 800 snails froze to death because of a faulty temperature control device. During the COVID lockdown, Department of Conservation rangers working in isolation continued to care for the snail population in refrigeration, feeding them worms and regularly changing the moss. There are nearly 2000 of them still living in refrigerators, and 10,000 captive snails and eggs have been released back into new areas around the mine.

Giant land snail, genus Powelliphanta.

INTRODUCED ANIMALS

Animals, birds, fish, reptiles and invertebrates lived in Aotearoa New Zealand for millennia before humans arrived. There were aerial predators, like eagles, falcons and harrier hawks, that hunted mostly during the day by sight, but the native creatures evolved to avoid them, becoming nocturnal like kiwi, or developing camouflage like kākāpō.

Then humans arrived, bringing mammal predators that hunt by scent. These defence strategies no longer worked and native creatures became very vulnerable to attack.

The environment changed drastically during the eighteenth and nineteenth centuries. Whalers and sealers plundered the seas. Māori had removed or burnt off a lot of native forest, but now tree felling, burning vegetation and clearing land for farming destroyed more native species' habitats. Draining wetlands led to the loss of 90% of the original wetlands area. The ships carrying new settlers brought plants and animals that would further change the landscape.

Settlers burning felled trees, 1856.

Forests and tussock went up in flames to clear the land for grazing and browsing animals like cattle and sheep.

Farmers used new, imported plant species, instead of native plant cover, as pasture. Animal pests were introduced, on purpose or by accident, and so were other plants that spread and became weeds. The speed of transformation was breathtaking and native plants, animals and birds were soon under threat from the new arrivals.

The introduction of plants and animals was carried out in a haphazard way, with no overall policy or planning. Travellers, families, ships' captains and crew and acclimatisation societies brought them into the country with no coordination between regions, and no understanding of the impact on the environment and existing ecosystems.

Why were these species introduced?	
Accidental introduction	White butterflies, German wasps
Biological control (to target other animals)	Insectivorous birds, stoats, ferrets, weasels
Companions or pets	Cats, dogs
Food and farming	Pigs, sheep, cows, goats, poultry
Fur industry	Possums
Nostalgia (reminders of home)	Sparrows, thrushes, blackbirds, starlings, hedgehogs
Pollinators	Bumblebees
Self-introduced (found their own way)	Rats, mice, monarch butterflies, birds
Sport and hunting	Deer, wapiti, chamois, tahr, trout, wallaby, hares, rabbits
Transport	Horses, bullocks

Some animals fall into more than one category. Rabbits were introduced for food and hunting, however selling their skins and tinning the meat grew into important industries. The black swan was introduced as a game bird, but also to control watercress that was choking the river Avon in Christchurch, and swan eggs were sold by the North Canterbury Acclimatisation Society.

Some introduced species didn't last long. The proposed silkworm industry didn't take off. Guinea pigs have never thrived in the wild (although they are kept as pets). Sir George Grey bought

LEFT The first cow and bull in the Nelson area, owned by farmer and stock trader Donald McGregor Drummond, around 1842.

RIGHT Parma wallaby, *Macropus parma.*

Kawau Island in 1862 during his second term as governor and made it into a private zoo, with kangaroos, wallabies, monkeys, antelopes, deer, emu, peacocks, cassowaries, kookaburra and even zebra. Many of his animals did not survive, but kookaburras and wallabies can still be seen in that area.

Thousands of birds, moths, butterflies, insects and spiders still regularly fly or are blown here. In the 1970s and 1980s, Ken Fox, a doctor from Manaia, collected insects that were blown across the Tasman Sea by strong westerly winds, including 36 species of Australian moths caught in light traps on offshore oil drilling platforms.

Tiger moth, *Utetheisa pulchelloides vaga*. One of the moths recorded by Ken Fox.

Birds are classed as native species if they arrived (often from Australia) on their own, without human help. The silvereye or wax-eye is called tauhou or 'new arrival' in te reo Māori. Like the welcome swallow/warou, it might have been blown off course while migrating. The royal spoonbill/kōtuku ngutupapa was first seen at Castlepoint in 1861. The white-faced heron/matuku moana arrived in the 1940s but is now our most common heron.

The monarch butterfly came from the other direction. It wasn't known outside North America until 1840, but after that it gradually spread west, probably by island-hopping across the Pacific. Monarch butterflies live on milkweed (like swan plants, a South African native popular in New Zealand). The plants they fed on in the Pacific might have sprouted from dried milkweed floss, once used to fill pillows and mattresses on ships, and as a substitute for kapok (a fibre no longer available but regularly used during the Second World War in lifejackets for US troops).

If storms and winds become stronger and fiercer in the future, it's possible that more new species will turn up, although our climate stops many from becoming established. The Australian painted lady butterfly regularly appears here and even lays eggs but can't survive the winter. A flock of pelicans was a surprising sight on the Kaipara Harbour in 2012, with the last recorded sighting in 2015.

Australian painted lady, *Vanessa kershawi*.

Australian pelicans, *Pelecanus conspicillatus.*

TO THE EDITOR OF THE LYTTELTON TIMES.

SIR,—A movement is now being made towards the formation of an acclimatisation society and subscriptions have been promised to a considerable amount. I have been requested to take a part in the matter, and I do not see that I can do so better than by attempting to enlist the support of the general public by giving all the information I can upon the subject, with the joint view of eliciting further information from others and of laying down the general features of acclimatisation for the benefit of those who have never bestowed much thought upon the matter.

The proposal is, in fact, to open a natura history class for the benefit of the community and to convert a portion of the rather howling-looking common of Hagley Park into a park for the people, a horticultural garden for the province, and further to enrich its interest by making it a nucleus for the reception of animals, including birds and fishes, whose introduction may be useful to the colony, and from whence they may be distri-

Excerpts from letters to the editor of the *Lyttelton Times* advocating for an acclimatisation society.

ACCLIMATISATION SOCIETIES

Acclimatisation, or introducing plants and animals to a new environment, was a fashionable movement in the nineteenth century. New migrants brought familiar plants and seeds with them to New Zealand. They also brought birds, animals and fish for farming and trade, hunting and fishing, transport, and as pets and reminders of home.

The first acclimatisation society in New Zealand was probably in Nelson, set up in 1863, but others soon followed. They were semi-private organisations, funded first by subscriptions and later by licence fees for fishing and hunting, and run by men who were prominent in their local communities. Few women were involved; hunting and fishing were mostly male sports.

The societies' aim was to introduce plants and animals to feed families and communities, supply clothing, create power and wealth in the form of farms and other revenue as well as provide a sentimental link to homes left behind. They introduced birds, rabbits, wallabies and possums. Transporting fish was difficult, but trout and salmon were brought here by packing fish ova (eggs) in moss and ice on board ship; the eggs were hatched and released into rivers.

The resulting changes happened quickly. George Malcolm Thomson wrote *The naturalisation of animals and plants in New Zealand* (1922), describing hundreds of species of mammals, birds, fish, reptiles, insects and invertebrates. He was critical of how everyone involved in introducing new species — societies, districts and individuals — had acted independently of each other, with no overall plan. Thomson said the history of acclimatisation efforts was full of 'bungles and blunders'.

In *Tutira: the story of a New Zealand sheep station,* William Herbert Guthrie-Smith recorded when introduced animals first turned up on his sheep run (stoats in 1921, hedge sparrows in 1922) and how native bird life plummeted. Some societies began to pay out bounties, or reward money, on animals classed as pests such as hedgehogs, ferrets and harrier hawks. Hedgehogs were introduced to deal with slugs and snails, but also fed on lizards, wētā and birds' eggs. Between 1922 and 1942, the Auckland society paid out on nearly a quarter of a million hawks, because they preyed on game birds. Eel drives were held because eels were thought to prey on ducks and trout.

TARANAKI ACCLIMATISATION SOCIETY.

VERMIN BONUSES.

FROM November 1, 1939, Bonuses at the following amended rates will be paid at the office of this Society, Bank of New South Wales Buildings, New Plymouth:
For tails of stoats, ferrets, weasels and polecats, two shilling (2/-); hedgehog snouts, 3d each; hawks' feet, 6d pair.

T. D. WEBSTER,
Secretary.

Bounty advertisement for stoats, ferrets, weasels, polecats, hedgehog snouts and hawks' feet.

Hedgehog snouts, ferret, stoat and weasel tails and the beaks or feet of hawks had to be provided as proof to claim the bounty. In 1940, a boy from Greytown sent in a sack of 125 hedgehog snouts, caught by his two fox terriers; he planned to use the bounty money to buy his first fishing licence.

Acclimatisation societies were disbanded in 1990. They became fish and game councils, overseeing hunting and fishing. Today there are strict rules about what you can and can't bring into the country. Animals that can never be imported because of risks to the environment include squirrels, foxes, cane toads, beavers, moles and snakes.

LIVESTOCK AND DOMESTIC ANIMALS

PIGS, CATTLE AND HORSES

French explorer Captain Jean de Surville gave two pigs to Māori in Doubtless Bay in 1769, and Captain Cook also released pigs into the bush on some of his visits. The wild pigs known as 'Captain Cookers' are thought to be descendants of Cook's pigs.

Tuki, one of two young men kidnapped in 1793 in the mistaken belief that they could teach convicts on Norfolk Island how to prepare flax, returned from Australia with gifts of ten sows

Captain Cook pig, *Sus scrofa*.

and two boars. In 1805, Te Pahi and his son Matara received more sows and boars from the governor of New South Wales after they had visited Port Jackson (now Sydney).

Cows and horses were unknown in the Bay of Islands when missionary Samuel Marsden brought some with him on the *Active* in 1814. John Liddiard Nicholas, in his *Narrative of a voyage to New Zealand,* described how the waiting crowd were bewildered and amazed by 'such extraordinary looking animals'. They scattered when one of the cows got loose and

Enderby Island cattle

Enderby Island cattle, one of the world's rarest cattle breeds, survived on seaweed, scrub and southern rata on the isolated sub-Antarctic Auckland Islands. They descended from cattle taken there by settlers as part of a failed farming attempt and were thought to be extinct after a culling operation to protect the native vegetation, but one last cow, named Lady, and her calf were rescued and shipped back to the mainland in 1993. The calf died but scientists saved the breed by using artificial breeding techniques such as embryo transplants and cloning. There are now three small flocks, about 30 animals in total.

Enderby Island cattle, *Bos taurus.*

stared in wonder at Samuel Marsden riding the horse along the beach. 'To see a man seated on the back of such an animal, they thought the strangest thing in nature.'

GOATS

The *Endeavour* on Cook's first voyage carried an English milch goat to give the captain and officers fresh milk. This goat had already been around the world on another ship and is thought to have spent the rest of her life in Cook's family backyard in Whitby.

Arapawa goat, *Capra aegagrus hircus.*

On his second and third voyages, Cook released goats into the bush on Arapawa Island. By 1977, there were 1000 to 1500 wild goats living there. The Forest Service carried out regular culls, but other people wanted to protect them as a gift to Māori from Captain Cook and a unique part of New Zealand's history.

Goats are browsing animals and farmers used them to keep weeds under control. In 1924, the government offered a £10,000 reward for a way to eradicate blackberry, originally introduced for food and hedges, but nobody claimed it and there were no solutions apart from goats. Goats that escaped from their herds could start feral populations of wild goats. Guthrie-Smith wrote about the difficult decision to use goats to save his farm, Tutira, from 'the devouring plague of blackberry'. He predicted that 'except on actual cliffs and precipices', every tree or bush would be stripped bare and there would be nowhere left for native birds to live.

Kaimanawa horses

Wild Kaimanawa horses have lived on the volcanic plateau in the central North Island for about 150 years. They descend from ponies imported and bred here by early European settlers, as well as other horses that have escaped or been released into the area, including military horses from the army camp at Waiouru set free to escape an infectious illness in 1941. The Department of Conservation carries out an annual muster and keeps herd numbers down to 300 to protect the fragile ecosystem against damage by their hooves and their grazing. Surplus horses can go to new homes and are popular because they are intelligent, tough and adaptable but also good natured.

Kaimanawa horses, *Equus ferus caballus.*

SHEEP

In the 1850s, thousands of sheep were taken by ship and then on foot to the south and east of the South Island. New settlers who had leased land from the government became wealthy station owners. In Canterbury alone, the total number of sheep increased in ten years (1858 to 1867) from 500,000 to two and a half million.

Wool made up nearly half of all exports by monetary value in 1880. It was valuable because it brought good prices and didn't spoil on the long sea journey. The total number of sheep reached 20 million in the late 1890s and peaked at 70 million in 1982, but has dropped to about 23 million today, when there are cheaper alternatives to wool and the revenue might not even cover the costs of shearing the sheep.

LEFT Sheep at Taieri Lake Station, 1895.

RIGHT The *Dunedin*, initially used as an immigrant ship, was one of the first ships to carry frozen meat between New Zealand and England.

In the early days of farming, it wasn't possible to export meat. But William Davidson, a Scotsman, knew about overseas experiments to carry refrigerated meat by ship. He had an immigrant sailing ship, the SS *Dunedin*, fitted with one of the new refrigeration machines. On 15 February 1882, it sailed from Port Chalmers carrying 5000 mutton, lamb and pig carcasses and over 2000 sheep tongues.

In the heat of the tropics, the cooling system stopped working. Captain John Whitson crawled into the hold to saw some holes for better air circulation. The *Dunedin* arrived in London in May with an unspoiled cargo. 'The sheep came out of their bags as bright as newly-killed mutton, and were declared by the Smithfield salesmen to be simply perfection.' This opened up huge new overseas markets for frozen meat and dairy products, and changed the economic future of the country.

Number of sheep, cattle and horses in New Zealand 1851–61

	1851	1858	1861
Sheep	233,043	1,523,324	2,760,183
Cattle	34,787	137,204	193,150
Horses	2890	14,912	28,270

(Statistics NZ, Statistics of New Zealand for 1861)

Depiction of a sheep being attacked by a kea, 1882.

SHEEP AND KEA

The kea is the world's only mountain parrot and famous for its bold, cheeky nature. In 1867, rumours spread that kea were attacking live sheep on high country stations in the South Island. The government introduced a bounty system, which local councils paid out on receipt of kea beaks or heads. Some 'rogue' kea might have been sheep killers, but more than 150,000 were killed as a result. Tricky methods were used to entice them, such as lacing sheep carcasses or skins with poison or intentionally wounding one bird to attract others.

Killing the kea was outlawed in 1970 in national parks, reserves and forests. It was not fully protected until 1986, the last native bird to be so.

DOGS

Early shepherds often brought their own dogs with them, especially border collies. Today's heading dogs or 'eye dogs', which can round up sheep without barking, are descended from the border collie.

Dogs and rabbits, Rock and Pillar Range, 1899.

Surveyors, rabbiters, explorers, hunters and farmers all kept dogs. Andreas Reischek's dog

Caesar could bring him birds and even butterflies alive and undamaged. Charlie 'Mr Explorer' Douglas would send his dog Topsy ahead in thick bush to try and work out a way through.

Poster for a dog tax imposed by the Hokianga County Council in the 1890s.

In 1880, the government passed a law that anyone who owned a dog had to pay a licence fee. This led to protests in the Hokianga, sometimes called the Dog Tax Rebellion, among a group of northern Māori led by Hōne Riiwi Tōia. Their hunting dogs were communally owned, and they couldn't afford to pay the tax. On 5 May 1898, 150 government militia marched on the Mahurehure settlement in Waimā but Māori leaders persuaded the group to surrender. Hōne Tōia and four others were sentenced to hard labour at Mount Eden Prison.

CATS

Cats are the most popular animal for household ownership in New Zealand.

Johann Forster, a German naturalist, was the scientist on Cook's second voyage, with his son Georg as his assistant. In *A voyage around the world in his Britannic majesty's sloop Resolution*, Georg wrote that the small birds would hop up close and even perch on the end of shotguns, so the men didn't want to shoot them. But the ship's cat had no such worries, and she 'took a walk in the woods every morning, and made great havoc among the little birds, that were not aware of such an insidious enemy'.

Ships' cats often escaped and went feral, but the story of the Stephens Island wren proved that even domestic cats could be dangerous predators.

The Stephens Island wren, also known as Lyall's wren, evolved to be flightless. After the kiore arrived, its habitat shrank until it was limited to Stephens Island/Takapourewa, near the western entrance to Cook Strait/Raukawa.

The Stephens Island lighthouse opened in January 1894. One of the keepers was David Lyall who brought his family and their cat Tibbles, pregnant with a litter of kittens.

Lyall noticed some unusual songbirds that looked like little mice as they scuttled around the rocks or jumped about in the scrub. They were too quick for him to catch, but not for Tibbles the cat. Lyall sent one specimen killed by Tibbles to Walter Buller and sold others to Henry Travers, a Wellington trader who sold them on to Walter Rothschild, a wealthy collector in England. Rothschild gave it the name *Traversia lyalli*, after Travers and Lyall.

But by the time the bird was named, in December 1894, there were very few, if any, left. The *Press* of 16 March 1895 called this 'probably a record performance in the way of extermination'.

Wild cats remained a problem on Stephens Island/Takapourewa for years. A new keeper shot more than 100 cats in ten months in 1899, but it wasn't until 1925 that the island was cat-free again. Tuatara, Hamilton's frog and giant wētā managed to survive and still live on the island.

Today there are fewer than 20 specimens of the Stephens Island wren held in museums in New Zealand and around the world. There are thought to be millions of feral cats in New Zealand, killing untold numbers of native birds.

LEFT Stephens Island wren, *Traversia lyalli*, 1895.
RIGHT Stephens Island wren, *T. lyalli*, a museum specimen at World Museum, Liverpool, England.

One of New Zealand's native bees, *Nesocolletes fulvescens.*

Bumblebee, genus Bombus.

BEES

Native bees, birds and lizards are important for pollination and seed dispersal of native plants. Lizards carry pollen on their skin and, like birds, they eat and disperse seeds. Honey-eaters like tūī, bellbird/korimako and stitchbird/hihi also pollinate flowers.

But when the new pasture crops were introduced, they could not be pollinated by native bees, which have a short proboscis or tongue. Red clover had to be re-sown every year until bumblebees, which are long-tongued, were introduced in 1885.

The first honeybees arrived with Mary Bumby who came to the Māngungu Mission Station, Hokianga, in 1839 with her brother John, a Wesleyan missionary. She brought two hives of bees and kept them alive through the long sea journey.

PESTS AND PREDATORS

RATS AND MICE

The large Norway or brown rat lived in ports and harbours and infested the ships of the early European explorers, whalers and sealers. These rats swarmed ashore along mooring ropes and proved hungry and vicious killers. The smaller ship or black rat arrived on settlers' ships; it was good at climbing trees and produced many litters a year, putting even more birds at risk.

Ship rat, *Rattus rattus.*

The first recorded house mice came off the *Elizabeth Henrietta*, a ship from Australia that ran ashore in 1824 on Ruapuke Island, south of Bluff. Local Māori were said to have called them 'hinereta' after the ship. Māori also gave it

Grey mouse in a South Island forest.

the name 'toronaihi' — after the whaler's knife used to slice up whale blubber — because of its sharp teeth.

Nelson and Marlborough were overrun with rats in 1884. The rats swam in wells and streams, making the water unfit for drinking. They climbed trees, destroyed crops and swarmed through kitchens and bedrooms. The *Nelson Evening Mail* of 8 December 1884 described how 'living rats are sneaking in every corner, scuttling across every path; their dead bodies in various stages of decay ... strew the roads, fields, and gardens.'

Today rats are still a problem, especially in mast years. Mast is the seed produced by beech trees, and in mast years, beech trees produce more flowers and enormous quantities of seed. This provides extra food for birds and insects but leads to a big increase in the population of rats and mustelids because they also have extra food available.

RABBITS

In Europe, there were predators to keep rabbits under control. In New Zealand, where their main predator was the hawk, their numbers skyrocketed, especially in the dryer, eastern regions of both islands. Rabbits were a source of fresh food and income for many families but they were hungry eaters, turning huge stretches of land into barren desert, covering them with dung, stripping the vegetation cover down to bare land and putting hillsides at risk of erosion.

The first rabbits were released in 1838 with more in the 1840s and 1850s, but they were fancy breeds that didn't survive. Wild rabbits came later. Four rabbits were brought on an immigrant ship from Scotland and set free near Invercargill in 1863. The *Otago Daily Times* of 15 July 1867 reported that the wild rabbits landed at Sandy Point had spread many miles inland and along the coast and 'it is quite a common thing to see men about the town with large and well-filled baskets of wild rabbits for sale'.

The rabbit plague

The Keene brothers owned an inland Kaikoura sheep run. In the early 1860s, one of the brothers released a pair of rabbits and within a few years, the run that had supported 20,000 sheep carried half that number of starving animals. The tussock was 'so eaten down as to resemble the stump of a worn out paintbrush' and the sheep only stayed alive 'by stripping the manuka scrub, and chewing flax'. Other farmers in the area found it nearly impossible to grow crops. The Keenes walked off the land in 1882.

Hundreds of rabbiters made their living from catching rabbits and skins were soon being exported in their thousands, from 3000 in 1873 to three million in 1878. In 1881, rabbit skins were the seventh most important export item after wool, gold, wheat, kauri gum, oats and tallow. By 1888, the total was 12 and a half million and in 1925 it reached 20 million.

Industries based on rabbit skins and frozen carcasses were booming. But as rabbit numbers increased, the number of animals that a farm could support dropped.

Farmers tried many solutions: using poisoned grain, releasing cats, employing rabbiters to shoot or trap them, or fumigating the warrens where rabbits lived. A runholder in Southland, where rabbits had been unknown three years before, had to employ 16 rabbiters and 120 dogs to try and get the numbers under control;

Rabbit skins being graded, 1930s.

36,000 rabbits were killed in one year, but still they multiplied.

In 1876, farmers and runholders told a government select committee that they were getting less wool and fewer lambs because ewes were malnourished. The committee's report suggested introducing weasels as a natural check to the rabbit problem. A series of Rabbit Nuisance Acts and amendments followed. Rabbit District Boards were set up, under rabbit inspectors. There were fines for killing weasels and stoats, and the building of rabbit proof fences (which didn't work) became widespread.

The Rabbit Destruction Council was set up in 1947. Myxomatosis, a disease caused by a virus, had helped to keep rabbit numbers down in Australia and was introduced here in 1950–51 but didn't work because there was no insect carrier or vector to spread it. New forms of aerial poisoning and the Rabbits Amendment Act 1956 (which ended the rabbit industry by banning the sale of skins and meat) led to reduced numbers however this was only temporary.

Rabbit calicivirus disease (RCD) spread

across Australia in 1995–96. The Ministry of Agriculture refused an application to release it here, saying it was too risky and might jump species. Despite this it was found on a farm in Central Otago in 1997, smuggled into the country by persons (or farmers) unknown. The disease spread and thousands of rabbits died; RCD is still here but with developing resistance, rabbit numbers are increasing again.

MUSTELIDS

Stoats, weasels and ferrets are members of the mustelid family, sharing the same shape — a long, thin body, short legs and pointed heads — and all stealthy and vicious killers. Ferrets are the largest, with males up to 44 cm long. They prefer open country and live on rabbits and hares but also target lizards, frogs, insects and ground-nesting birds. Stoats will live anywhere, and are strong swimmers and agile tree climbers. Weasels are the smallest, up to 20 cm long, and their flexible bodies can slither through thumb-sized gaps.

These animals were introduced by the government in the 1870s and 1880s in the hope of controlling rabbit numbers. Sir George Grey tried to ban their import because he realised they would be harmful to birds. In Parliamentary debates on 25 October 1876, some MPs agreed with him but not Captain Fraser, an Otago farmer. 'It was all very well for gentlemen who were not suffering from the rabbit pest ... He himself was very fond of birds, but if it came to be a question whether he would have birds or sheep, he would certainly vote in favour of the sheep.' The MPs voted against Grey's proposal, deciding that the wool industry was more important than birds.

Ferret, *Mustela furo*.

Stoat, *Mustela erminea*.

It wasn't easy to transport such fierce and bloodthirsty creatures by ship. Henry Allbone and his son Walter collected stoats, weasels and ferrets from English gamekeepers and travelled to New Zealand many times, bringing the animals in cages. They also carried live pigeons as food on the voyage.

Thousands of stoats, weasels and ferrets were released however they didn't control rabbit numbers and had a terrible impact on native birds, eating eggs, killing chicks and competing with adult birds for food. Today no one is allowed to farm, breed or sell ferrets, stoats or weasels, except with a special permit. In some countries ferrets are kept as pets, but that was banned here in 2002, in case any pet ferrets escaped.

POSSUMS

The common brushtail possum was introduced from Australia to Southland in 1837 (when they didn't survive) and again in 1858. It was protected under the Animals Protection Act 1907 for the sake of the valuable fur trade; in 1926, 155,000 skins were sent to market.

Brushtail possum, *Trichosurus vulpecula.*

A 1920 report concluded that possums caused 'negligible' damage to native forests. But it acknowledged they did harm to orchards and gardens, and it was partly for that reason that the government made it illegal in 1921 to import more possums.

Over the following years, the damage possums caused became clear, and in 1946 they were declared a pest and no longer protected. For ten years, from 1951 to 1961, the government ran a bounty scheme, which paid out two shillings and sixpence on proof of the possum's ears and a strip of fur. In the 1960s, possums were found to be carrying and infecting cattle and deer with bovine tuberculosis (TB) and there were more efforts to control possum numbers, using trapping and poisons in bait stations on the ground or dropped by helicopter.

Today there are millions of possums, eating their way steadily through leaves, fruit and flowers (up to 21,000 tonnes of vegetation a night) as well as birds, eggs, insects and snails.

CATERPILLARS VERSUS SPARROWS

Caterpillars, crickets, grasshoppers and other insects were a serious problem for farmers from the 1860s on. One newspaper reported that an 'army of caterpillars' invaded a patch of land on the West Coast, 'and in a day or two ate every blade of grass as completely as if the ground had been burnt'.

Native birds retreated to the bush as the land was cleared. To farmers and acclimatisation societies, the obvious solution was to import insect-eating birds to control the insects.

It wasn't easy to keep birds alive on the long sea voyage from the UK. Often they moulted in the hot weather of the tropics and froze to death in the colder southern seas. In 1867 and 1868,

House sparrow, *Passer domesticus*.

Captain Stevens of the *Matoaka* brought pheasants, partridges, larks, green linnets, chaffinches, starlings, blackbirds, thrushes and sparrows to Lyttelton for the Canterbury Acclimatisation Society.

The Otago and other acclimatisation societies ordered birds from Richard Bills and his son Charles, who travelled seven times to New Zealand, bringing hundreds of birds. A passenger on the *Warrior Queen* in 1871 described the deckhouse full of cages and barrels of birdseed and worms.

Sparrows controlled the caterpillar menace, but sparrow numbers soared out of control and caused their own problems. Sparrow Clubs were formed to encourage boys to collect sparrows and their eggs. The Woodend and Waikuku sparrow clubs counted over 2000 eggs and 200 birds at one meeting, with 500 eggs collected by one boy.

Caterpillars even caused havoc on train lines. In February 1883, trains from Waverley were brought to a halt because caterpillars slithered over the tracks and made them so greasy that the wheels couldn't grip the rails. Train officials had to sweep and sand the tracks before the trains could continue.

Colin Miskelly walked the 3000-km tramping trail Te Araroa over the summer of 2023–24, counting birdlife along the way. The most common birds were sparrows. He counted 12,500 in total, twice as many as the next most common birds (chaffinch and red-billed gull), including over 1000 on one day in south Auckland.

PLAGUE OF CATEPILLARS.

STOP A TRAIN

(Per Press Association.)

WELLINGTON, this day.

The train which left Wanganui yesterday afternoon a few miles from Fordell encountered millions of caterpillars crossing the railway line, the objective being a field of oats. The train was stopped through the wheels skidding, till sand was used.

GAME ANIMALS

In Britain, the rich and titled controlled access to forests, fields and streams. New settlers would not face such barriers to hunting and fishing here, if only there were enough animals to hunt or catch.

The Tourist and Health Resorts Department was set up under Thomas Donne in 1901. Tourism would bring in money through licence fees, the employment of guides, and the need for food and transport. The department's 1903 annual report said sport attracted overseas visitors and New Zealand ought to become 'one of the foremost of the sporting countries in the world'.

DEER

Hunter carrying a deer, 1920s.

Red deer were introduced for hunting from the 1850s. With plenty of food and no predators, huge herds were soon doing enormous damage to forests, browsing all the vegetation they could reach. The 1922 Forest Service annual report admitted deer were rapidly becoming a nuisance. Alan Perham's 1922 report on deer in New Zealand, and the damage they were doing, estimated there were 300,000 of them.

In the 1930s, the government took all protection off wild deer. Deer cullers were strong, fit, self-reliant and expert bushmen. They lived in tents or caves for months with little contact with the outside world, carrying heavy packs full of ammunition, their sleeping bag and basic food supplies.

During the Second World War, little ammunition was available and the deer culling programme was cut back, but between 1930 and 31 March 1956 when the Forest Service took it over, nearly 700,000 deer were killed. Meanwhile the overseas market for wild venison and deer velvet took off. Hunters began to shoot deer from helicopters, and later to capture live animals with tranquiliser guns or net guns for commercial deer farms, making big money but also running big risks in the mountains.

In 1997, the Department of Conservation estimated there were 250,000 wild deer. Deer

Poster advertising sport hunting in New Zealand, 1930s.

had been culled for over 60 years, but there were still almost as many deer as the 300,000 that Perham estimated in 1922.

MOOSE

Ten Canadian moose were brought in crates across the Pacific Ocean and released at Supper Cove in Dusky Sound, Fiordland, in April 1910. This followed an unsuccessful attempt to release moose near Hokitika in 1900; ten died in a storm on the voyage and the other four only survived for a few years.

Moose, or signs of them, were glimpsed over the following years, but no one knew how many there were, how far they had spread or how they were affected by the growing herds of red deer.

The last photograph of a moose was taken

Importation of big game to New Zealand, 1910.

in 1952, but unconfirmed sightings continued. Ken Tustin, scientist and helicopter pilot, spent years talking to people who had (or thought they had) seen moose: hunters, fishermen and helicopter crews. A 1972 Moose Survey in Fiordland found a cast antler that might only have been a year or two old. Tustin kept searching, camping and tramping and setting up cameras in remote areas. He never saw a moose, but believed he found evidence they still existed: not only their browsing patterns (moose are enormous, up to two metres tall, and can reach far higher up trees than deer) but also large footprints, and hair samples proved by DNA testing in 2001 to come from moose.

Hunter with moose, Fiordland, early 1900s.

WAPITI, TAHR AND CHAMOIS

In 1905, the Tourist Department sent inspector Fred Moorhouse to the United States to collect game animals. Moorhouse brought back a menagerie that included birds (horned owls, Canadian geese, snow geese, mandarin ducks and wood ducks), raccoons, deer and North American elk, also known as wapiti.

Ten wapiti were gifts from President Roosevelt, and the ducks, raccoons and owls were gifts from the Washington Zoological Gardens. The rest were bought at the St. Louis World's Fair.

The wapiti were taken to Fiordland on board the government steamer *Hinemoa* and released into George Sound. Moorhouse went back in 1921 and could tell from tracks and sightings that the population was thriving. Today's Fiordland wapiti deer are a cross between the original wapiti and red deer.

The Duke of Bedford gifted five Himalayan tahr and six Japanese deer from his English estate that were released at Mt Cook/Aoraki and the Kaimanawa Range. Chamois were a gift from the Emperor of Austria, in return for live native birds, and were also released at Mt Cook/Aoraki.

LEFT Chamois, *Rupicapra rupicapra.*

RIGHT Wapiti, *Cervus canadensis.*

These large game animals are browsers that feed on grasses, plants and leaves and bark of trees, stripping native forests of vegetation. But they are also valued by hunters, especially the wapiti for their large antlers, and differing opinions between hunting groups and conservationists over the best way to manage the herds and control their population has led to fierce debate and disagreements.

GROUSE

John Cullen, first warden of Tongariro National Park, wanted to introduce grouse in the park for sport. Grouse are large game birds and were hunted on English and Scottish moors, where they feed on heather. Cullen scattered imported heather seeds through the tussock between 1912 and 1922. The 'Heather and Grouse' controversy caused fierce debates over whether the heather would crowd out native plants. (Cullen said it wouldn't.) The grouse didn't survive the harsh climate but the heather became a pest weed, pushing out the native tussock.

PEST CONTROL

Plants and animals might be introduced on purpose or by accident, but what happened next often followed a common pattern. The new species thrived so well that farmers and scientists were soon looking for ways to control them. This was especially important when they threatened to affect farm production.

White butterflies were probably brought in as larvae or pupae on board a ship. In March 1930, one was spotted over flower beds in a bowling green in Napier; a week later, another was seen in the grounds of Napier Boys' High School. The white butterfly targets vegetable crops like cabbages, cauliflower, turnips and kale, grown as feed for cattle and sheep and in market and home gardens, so it posed a serious threat. By 1933, fluttering white clouds of butterflies hovered in their millions over roadsides and pasture in Hawke's Bay. By 1935, they had spread across the North Island and reached the South Island as well.

When new species were introduced it always altered the balance of nature that had existed for millennia before humans arrived. One option for dealing with species that become pests (animals) or weeds (plants) is biological control. This means identifying and importing another new species — a natural enemy that might control their spread — in the way that ferrets, stoats and weasels were introduced to control rabbits.

Other options are chemical methods. DDT, an insecticide used against malarial mosquitoes in the Pacific in the Second World War, was added to aerial topdressing, although insects developed resistance and people became worried about its effect on human and animal health and the environment. DDT was banned from pastures in 1970, and completely in 1989.

New Zealand uses a big proportion (80–90%) of the world's production of 1080, or sodium fluoroacetate (1080 is the brand

White butterfly, *Pieris rapae*.

name), and this remains controversial. Hunters and animal rights groups alike claim the biodegradable bait pellets cause an inhumane death and can harm other animals like dogs, deer and pigs as well as damage the environment. In 2011 Dr Jan Wright, Parliamentary Commissioner for the Environment, released a report *Predators, poisons and silent forests*. She concluded that 1080 was 'the only practical and cost-effective option that is available for controlling possums, rats and stoats in large and inaccessible areas.'

'The possums, rats and stoats that have invaded our country will not leave of their own accord,' Dr Wright wrote. 'Much of our identity as New Zealanders, along with the clean green brand with which we market our country to the world, is based on the ecosystems these pests are bent on destroying. We cannot allow our forests to die'.

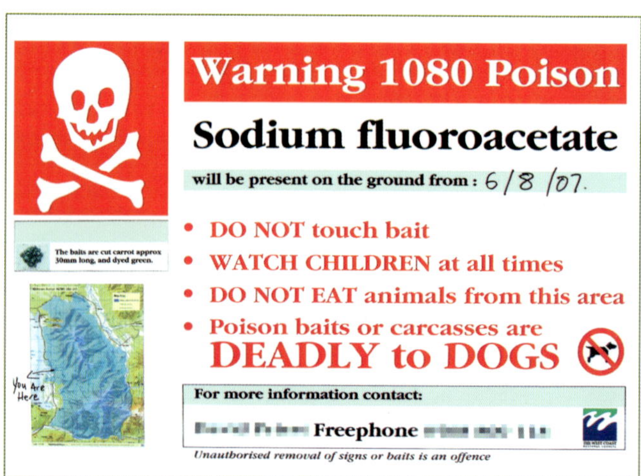

1080 poison warning sign.

ENTERTAINMENT VALUE

MASCOTS

Soldiers in both world wars took animals on board ship with them or found mascots overseas. Dogs, kangaroos, wallabies and monkeys provided amusement and reminders of home and were symbols of valued qualities like loyalty, endurance, compassion and bravery. Despite quarantine rules, some also managed to bring their mascots back.

Jacko was an Abyssinian monkey, acquired by New Zealand soldiers in Egypt, who went with them as their regimental pet to France. The French villagers had never seen a monkey before and only recognised him from pictures in books. Jacko survived Armentières and the Somme and was shown for a month in the London Zoological Gardens, but Sergeant Fabian was determined to bring him back to Wellington Zoo. 'Many French women tried to get him from me for a "souvenir," but ... I always had it in my mind that this was the most suitable place for Jacko to end his days.'

ZOOS AND CIRCUSES

The history of zoos and circuses in New Zealand is full of quirky stories, but it's also a mirror of changing social attitudes towards animals.

Auckland's first zoo was a private one, run by John James Boyd in Onehunga from 1911. Local people weren't happy about having a collection of lions, tigers, bears, monkeys, birds and deer in their suburb, and the Auckland City Council began to build its own zoo

An Otago soldier with the regimental monkey Jacko, who was taken from Cairo to Gallipoli.

near Western Springs Lake; it bought some of Boyd's animals and opened in 1922.

In 1925, a young female leopard from India slipped through the bars of her cage. Zookeepers advised there was little danger except to poultry, cats and dogs, nevertheless alarm and anxiety still gripped the city. The city council advertised a reward (£20 alive, £10 if dead), but three weeks after her escape she was found drowned in the harbour.

Other escapees included Faith, a young hippo who floated out of her enclosure when the creek flooded, Burma the elephant who broke out of her moated enclosure into Western Springs Park, leading to an armed offenders callout, and Jin, the Asiatic small-clawed otter. Jin was spotted on the North Shore and zookeepers drove around the streets looking for her. After four weeks, she was caught in a trap on Rangitoto Island and returned to the zoo.

Wellington Zoo opened in Newtown in 1906. Its first occupant was a lion, King Dick, named after Prime Minister Richard Seddon, and offered to the city by a travelling circus.

Other famous Wellington Zoo animals were the Antarctic sledge dogs. Osman was donated by school children for Captain Scott's last expedition. Once, when the dogs in his team fell down a crevasse, he kept his footing and held their weight until they could be saved. Oscar and three other sledge dogs pulled sledges for 1500 miles (2414 km) in 150 days for the Ross Sea party of Shackleton's 1914–17 expedition.

Wellington Zoo had its own escape artists. In 1967, two tigers, Napoleon and Josephine, got out of their enclosure when a zookeeper failed to lock a door properly. People saw them wandering through the dark streets of Newtown. Police, army and the fire brigade were called out and members of a travelling circus came to help. Tranquiliser darts didn't work and both tigers were shot and killed.

Early zoos had a focus on entertainment rather than animal welfare and conservation. Enclosures were small and cramped; in 1917, Ernest Joyce from the Shackleton expedition asked for better housing for the sledge dogs. Elephant rides and chimpanzee tea parties were popular in the 1950s and 1960s. Baby chimpanzees (sometimes in human clothing) were trained to sit in chairs, eat food set out on the table, pour tea from teapots and drink from teacups.

Entertainment was also part of Napier's Marineland, which opened in 1965 with six captured dolphins. Sea lions, sea leopards, fur seals and otters were on display, but the dolphins were the stars. Thousands of people came to watch them swim, dive and perform tricks. Marineland closed to the public in 2008 when the last captive dolphin died. It stayed open to care for sick and injured sea mammals but closed for good in 2015.

Travelling circuses toured the country during the nineteenth and twentieth century, moving their animals in cages and crates, at first in

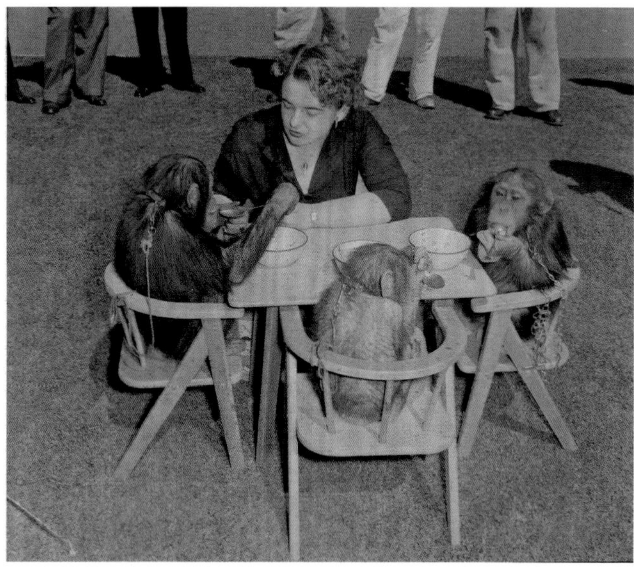

Chimpanzee tea party, Wellington Zoo, 1956.

horse-drawn wagons and later by train. Cooper and Bailey's Circus boasted 'the grandest beast collection on the face of the Globe'. This included bison, elk, elephants, camels, lions, tigers, zebras, hyenas, sea lions and leopards, as well as 'a Huge Black Hairy Rhinoceros (the only one ever captured alive)'. The circus put up tents in each new town and played to audiences of thousands. They left by ship from Auckland in May 1878, but unfortunately the elephant Titania, who had entertained audiences with her balancing tricks, died on

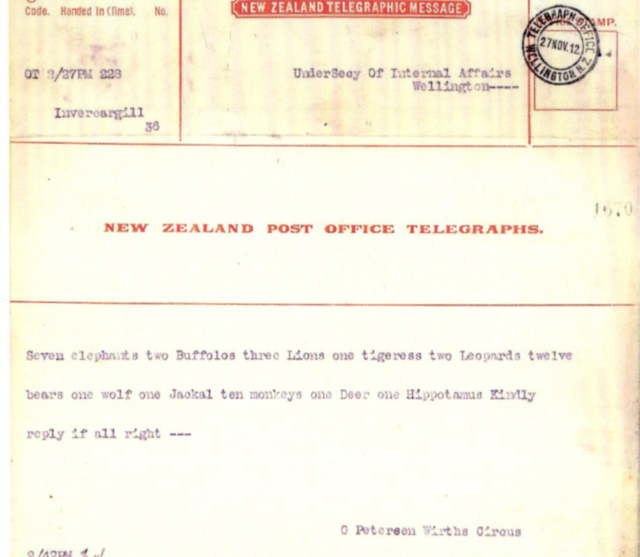
NEW ZEALAND TELEGRAPHIC MESSAGE

Code. Handed in (Time). No.

OT 2/27PM 228

Invercargill
36

UnderSecy Of Internal Affairs
Wellington----

27 NOV. 12 TELEGRAPH OFFICE WELLINGTON N.Z.

NEW ZEALAND POST OFFICE TELEGRAPHS.

Seven elephants two Buffolos three Lions one tigeress two Leopards twelve bears one wolf one Jackal ten monkeys one Deer one Hippotamus Kindly reply if all right ---

G Petersen Wirths Circus

2/42PM

Application from G. Peterson, Touring Manager, Wirth Bros Circus, for permit to land various circus animals.

Circus elephants walking toward Rugby League Park, Newtown, Wellington.

board after swallowing 'the contents of [a] man's pocket, including a large box of matches'.

Other circus elephants have died after eating tutu, a poisonous native shrub. Betty, the baby elephant in the Sole Brothers circus, survived eating tutu on the roadside between Awakino and Te Kuiti when her handlers were trying to rescue some monkeys, but died of pneumonia at the Epsom Showgrounds later in 1937.

The last two elephants in New Zealand were Auckland Zoo's Anjalee and Burma. Angalee arrived from an elephant orphanage in Sri Lanka in 2015, after being quarantined on Niue. Both elephants left for new homes in Australia when the zoo decided it could no longer create an elephant family herd.

ANIMAL CELEBRITIES

OPO the bottlenose dolphin lived in the waters off Opononi on the Hokianga harbour between mid-1955 and March 1956. Piwai Toi wrote in *Te Ao Hou* about seeing Opo in June 1955: 'Suddenly there was a big splash and a boiling swirl. A large fish was streaking

Opo at Opononi, 1956.

for my boat just under the surface. I really thought it was going to hit my boat, when about 10 yards away, it dived and surfaced on the other side. It played round and round the boat. Such was the way I first met Opo.' Hohepa Heperi, a local elder, told him, 'Opo is the fish of peace, a legacy from Kupe'. Opo played with people, especially children, letting them pat her and ride on her back, and performed flipping and balancing tricks with beach balls and bottles. Thousands of visitors flocked to see her. A special law was passed to give her official protection, but she was found dead in a rock pool on 9 March 1956 and buried by the War Memorial Hall. Films, books and songs were made about her and there is a statue of her in the town.

PELORUS JACK was a Risso's dolphin famous for meeting ships on the Nelson–Wellington run and swimming alongside them in French Pass, a dangerous stretch of water near the entrance to Pelorus Sound. He (or possibly she) regularly appeared between 1888 and 1912. James Cowan wrote in 1910 that local Māori called the dolphin Kaikai-a-waro, and believed he was a guardian and taniwha who lived in a sea cave and protected them when they went to sea. Pelorus Jack was spotted less often through 1912 and last seen at the end of that year. Two bulldogs later took the same name, the first a few months after Pelorus Jack was last seen, as mascots of the battlecruiser HMS *New Zealand*.

Prohibiting Taking of Risso's Dolphin in Cook Strait, &c.

Governor.

ORDER IN COUNCIL.

At the Government House, at Wellington, this 26th day of September, 1904.

Present:

HIS EXCELLENCY THE GOVERNOR IN COUNCIL.

WHEREAS it is enacted by section five of "The Sea-fisheries Act, 1894," that the Governor in Council may from time to time make regulations, which shall have general force and effect throughout the colony, or particular force and effect only in any waters or places specified therein, for, among other things, prohibiting altogether for such period as he shall think fit the taking of any fish, and may by such regulations impose a penalty for breach of such regulations:

And whereas it is desirable to prohibit the taking of the fish or mammal known as Risso's dolphin (*Grampus griseus*) in Cook Strait and the adjacent bays, sounds, and estuaries:

Now, therefore, His Excellency the Governor of the Colony of New Zealand, in exercise of the hereinbefore-recited power and authority, and acting by and with the advice and consent of the Executive Council of the said colony, doth hereby make the following regulations:—

REGULATIONS.

1. DURING the period of five years from the date of the gazetting of these regulations it shall not be lawful for any person to take the fish or mammal of the species commonly known as Risso's dolphin (*Grampus griseus*) in the waters of Cook Strait, or of the bays, sounds, and estuaries adjacent thereto.

2. Any person committing a breach of this regulation shall be liable to a penalty of not less than five pounds nor more than one hundred pounds.

Clerk of the Executive Council.

The order protecting Pelorus Jack.

MOKO was a bottlenose dolphin who lived between 2007 and 2010 first at Māhia Beach, then Waikanae Beach in Gisborne, Whakatāne and Tauranga. He had many playful encounters with swimmers and was famous for rescuing a stranded adult pygmy sperm whale and her calf by guiding them through a channel to the open sea. His dead body was found in 2010 washed up on Matakana Island, where he was buried. A sculpture of him is by the Whakatāne River.

PHAR LAP — his name came from the Thai word for 'sky flash' or 'lightning' — was a champion racehorse, bought for a bargain, who went on to win 37 of his 51 races. The public loved him because they saw him as a battler, and were

Taxidermy of Phar Lap in a glass case, on display at the Melbourne Museum.

inspired by his strength, courage and endurance. He was born in Timaru in 1926, trained and ran most of his races in Australia, and died suddenly in the USA in 1932. He had already survived being shot at and there were suggestions that he was poisoned. There is a statue of him in Timaru and his body parts are on display in three places: his skeleton at Te Papa Tongarewa in Wellington, his preserved heart — about twice the weight of the average horse's heart — at the National Museum of Australia in Canberra and his stuffed body at the Melbourne Museum.

CHARISMA, nicknamed Podge because he loved his food, was born in 1972. He was not a big horse but he was brave and easily trained, and took his rider Mark Todd to back-to-back Olympic gold in eventing at Los Angeles in 1984 and Seoul in 1988. The 1984 win was the first time the New Zealand equestrian teams had won gold in this category, a combination of dressage (following a set routine of challenges), show jumping and cross country. Charisma won many other competitions but was euthanased in 2003 after breaking a shoulder in an accident.

BESS was one of about 10,000 horses sold or donated to the government for overseas service in the First World War. Only four horses, including Bess, ever came back. Because of strict quarantine rules and not enough ships, all the others that survived to the end of the war had to be sold or shot. Her owner, Charles Guy Powles, put up a memorial to her near Bulls in Manawatū, where Anzac Day services are now held.

TORTY the tortoise came to New Zealand on the hospital ship *Marama* in 1916; she had scars on her shell from being run over by a gun wagon, but a New Zealand stretcher bearer had rescued her. Torty was living with descendants of the same family in 2022. She was once stolen for a circus, but a policeman recognised her scars and rescued her again.

MURPHY was one of several donkeys that belonged to John Simpson, a stretcher bearer with the Australian forces at Gallipoli, who used them to carry wounded soldiers down from the hills. Simpson was famous for his cheerful spirit even under fire, but on 19 May 1915 he was shot and killed, only three weeks after landing. War artist Horace Moore-Jones made a famous painting of Simpson and Murphy, but it was based on a photograph of Richard Henderson, a New Zealander, who also used donkeys to transport the wounded. In 1997, Murphy was awarded the RSPCA Purple Cross Award for animal bravery in war.

'Man with a donkey' by H. Moore-Jones.

SIROCCO the kākāpō was born on 23 March 1997 but became sick when a few weeks old. He was hand-raised for several months and then put on an island, however he had grown used to being around people and was comfortable in their company. This made him a perfect ambassador for kākāpō recovery, and he was taken around the country so people had the chance to meet one of these amazing birds. He spent the rest of the time on an offshore island and went missing in 2016 when his transmitter device failed, but he was found again two years later.

RICHARD HENRY the kākāpō was named after Richard Henry the conservationist who worked so hard to keep kākāpō and kiwi safe from predators. He was found high in the mountains of Fiordland in 1975. There were so few kākāpō left — no others were found in Fiordland — that he was moved to offshore islands in the hope he could help increase the kākāpō population and its genetic diversity with a mix of Fiordland and Stewart Island/Rakiura kākāpō genes. He had three chicks with Flossie in 1998 and died in 2010 when he might have been 80 years old.

Paddy the Wanderer, Wellington.

PADDY THE WANDERER began life as Dash, an Airedale terrier owned by the Glasgow family of Wellington, but after their little daughter Elsie died of pneumonia in 1928, he wandered away and became adopted by waterfront workers and seamen down at the wharves. Now named Paddy, he caught trams and taxis around the city and even went on several trips by ship. After he died in July 1939, his body was carried through the city by a procession of black taxi cabs. There is a memorial plaque by the Queens Wharf gates, next to a water fountain with drinking bowls for dogs. Paddy's dog registration fee is still paid every year by Wellington Museum.

MINSTREL, a black and white sheepdog, turned up as a six-month-old stray when poet Sam Hunt was living at Bottle Creek in Paremata. Sam and Minstrel toured the country for years for poetry readings and gigs. Minstrel featured in several of Sam Hunt's poems and on the cover of one of his books. Newspapers covered his death in 1988 with the headline 'N.Z.'s best known dog, Minstrel, dead'.

FRIDAY the sheep dog belonged to James Mackenzie, a Scottish shepherd, and it was said she only obeyed orders in Gaelic. In 1855, Mackenzie was on trial in Lyttelton Courthouse, accused (some said unfairly) of stealing sheep from a sheep station. He hardly spoke, but one later story said he sobbed with emotion when Friday was brought in as evidence: 'Eh, Lassie! Poor Lassie! They've got ye too!' Mackenzie was sent to prison but pardoned in 1856 and left the country; nobody knows what happened to him after that, or to his dog Friday.

CAESAR the bulldog was the mascot of the New Zealand Rifle Brigade in France in the First World War. (His name is spelt 'Ceaser' on his collar in the Auckland War Memorial Museum.) He was a Red Cross dog and wore a harness that contained bandages and water for wounded soldiers, and letter writing materials if they needed to send a message back to the trenches. Caesar was killed in the Battle of the Somme in 1916 and buried next to the soldier who died beside him. In 2019, he was awarded the Blue Cross Medal for his service and bravery.

MRS CHIPPY was a tabby cat on board the *Endurance*, the ship that Shackleton took to Antarctica in 1914. She was actually a male cat, called 'Mrs' by mistake, and belonged to the ship's chippy or carpenter, Harry McNeish, although he was a general favourite.

Statue of Mrs Chippy on Harry McNeish's grave in Wellington.

The *Endurance* became trapped in the ice and the crew could only take the essentials when they set off on a perilous journey across the ice. Shackleton wrote in his diary on 29 October 1915: 'This afternoon Sallie's three youngest pups, Sue's Sirius, and Mrs. Chippy, the carpenter's cat, have to be shot.' Harry McNeish died and was buried in Wellington in 1930 and a statue of Mrs Chippy sits on his grave.

HAPPY FEET was the second emperor penguin to come ashore here. The first one arrived at Oreti Beach, near Invercargill in April 1967 and was taken out to sea and released off Foveaux Strait. Happy Feet (tests later showed he was male)

Happy Feet.

was found on the beach at Peka Peka, Kāpiti, in June 2011. After several days, when he started to eat sticks and wet sand, he was taken to the hospital at Wellington Zoo, and later fitted with a satellite tracking device and returned to the Southern Ocean near Campbell Island. The tracking information showed that he swam about 100 km south in five days. Then the signals stopped, and no one knows what happened after that.

CLYDE the otter escaped from his enclosure at Wellington Zoo in 1999. Two days later, flatmates spotted him in their outside laundry, a kilometre away. Zookeepers set traps, however it took three more days before he was caught. A month later, Clyde found a way out again. He was caught inside the zoo grounds but it seemed that Wellington Zoo wasn't the best place for him, and he went to a new zoo home in Australia.

SHREK was a merino sheep from Bendigo Station, near Tarras, in Central Otago. For six years he avoided the musters for sheep shearing. When finally tracked down in 2004, he was so shaggy that he could hardly see, and his fleece — he was shorn live on TV — weighed 27 kg, six times heavier than average. Naming him after the ogre of the film was the suggestion of teenagers taking part in local Pony Club competitions. Later, Shrek met Prime Minister Helen Clark at Parliament and he was shorn for charity twice, once on a floating iceberg. He died in 2011, aged 16, and his mounted body and a jersey made from his wool are held at Te Papa Tongarewa; there is a bronze statue of him in Tarras.

Statue of Shrek.

SANCTUARIES AND CONSERVATIONISTS

Sanctuaries can be as big as an island or as small as the Cromwell Chafer Beetle Nature Reserve in Central Otago. This dry paddock was the first insect reserve in New Zealand, and possibly the world, and protects a large flightless beetle that burrows underground. The reserve is the only place the beetle is found, and it is under threat even there from redback spiders lurking in rabbit holes. An annual survey estimates its population by checking hundreds of core samples for beetle larvae.

Cromwell Chafer Beetle Nature Reserve, south of Cromwell, South Island.

Breaksea Island.

Other sanctuaries for small creatures include the Mahoenui Giant Wētā Scientific Reserve in King Country/Te Rohe Pōtae, the Mokomoko Dryland Sanctuary for lizards in Central Otago, and the predator-proof fence built around a stretch of disused gravel road in the Mackenzie Basin/Te Manahuna to protect the robust grasshopper.

New Zealand has more than 600 islands and over 100 are now pest free. Island sanctuaries were established from the 1890s on. Breaksea Island, Codfish Island/Whenua Hou, Mana, Kāpiti and Tiritiri Matangi were among those first cleared of rats using poison bait stations.

Hihi, *Notiomystis cincta*, on Tiritiri Matangi.

Little Barrier Island became New Zealand's first Nature Reserve in 1895. Under the Ngāti Manuhiri Claims Settlement Act 2012, the Crown acknowledged that its purchase of the island breached the Treaty of Waitangi and recognised Ngāti Manuhiri as kaitiaki of the Little Barrier Island Nature Reserve/Te Hauturu-o-Toi.

Big South Cape Island, southwest of Stewart Island/Rakiura, was home to many native birds and bats until rats arrived. In March 1964, muttonbirders landed for the annual harvest of tītī. They found the island swarming with rats and hardly any birds left. The Royal New Zealand Navy sent a wildlife team to try and rescue three bird species: the bush wren, South Island snipe and South Island saddleback. Waiting until the weather cleared so they could take the birds to a safe neighbouring island, the team fed the saddlebacks on leftover Christmas cake studded with dried fruit, which the birds picked out. The wren and snipe were harder to find and feed, and didn't survive — they are now extinct.

Campbell Island/Motu Ihupuku, one of the sub-Antarctic islands, was overrun with rats. In 2001, during the winter to avoid nesting birds, helicopters flew over and dropped tonnes of poison bait. Two years later, the island was declared rat-free. It had gone from being an island with the highest density of rats in the world, to the site of the biggest rat eradication programme in the world at that time.

Mercury Islands tusked wētā, *Motuweta isolata Johns.*

The Mercury Islands tusked wētā was only discovered in 1970 on Middle Island/Ātiu in the Mercury Islands group. Years of drought were threatening their habitat and scientists collected one male and two female wētā in 1998 to start a captive breeding programme. They were only just in time; no more tusked wētā have been found on Middle Island since 2001, but the ones descended from the three captive wētā saved the species from extinction and now live on other nearby islands.

The Mokohinau stag beetle is another endangered island-dwelling species. It lives in one small area of vegetation on a rocky outcrop called Stack H in the Mokohinau Islands and was noticed in the 1880s by a lighthouse keeper. Several searches have been carried out since the 1990s but few were found and it may now be extinct.

Mokohinau stag beetle, *Geodorcus ithaginis.*

Led by the vision of people like Jim Lynch, an old dam in the Wellington suburb of Karori was converted into Zealandia, a wildlife sanctuary in the middle of a city, surrounded by a predator-proof fence that was a world-first in design. Rats, cats, possums and ferrets were put on one side of a prototype fence built inside

Predator-proof fence, Zealandia.

Zealandia.

Hector's dolphin, *Cephalorhynchus hectori.*

a garage and filmed to see if they could jump or climb over, burrow under or squeeze through. Zealandia (since followed by other fenced mainland sanctuaries) has achieved mainland releases of little spotted kiwi/kiwi pukupuku and tuatara, breeding populations of threatened species and huge increases in numbers of native birds like tūī and kākā outside the fenced area.

Other sanctuaries are marine reserves, although these make up less than 1% of the waters around New Zealand. The Goat Island Marine Reserve was the first, established in 1977. The Banks Peninsula Marine Mammal Sanctuary was set up in 1988 to protect Hector's dolphins. In 2024, the Akaroa Marine Reserve hit the news when the first day's races for SailGP, a global race series for catamarans, were called off because of dolphin sightings in the harbour.

CONCLUSION

New Zealand's environment evolved for millions of years without people or large mammals, but changes began as soon as the first Polynesian voyagers arrived. Over the following centuries they dug, cleared and burned the land to make space for crops, villages and paths. Some fires may have spread out of control. Other areas became prone to soil erosion. Species of native birds and other creatures were driven to extinction by hunting, predation by kiore and kurī, and habitat loss.

The arrival of European settlers sped up this process. Colonisation involved animals and plants as well as people and changed the environment forever. Species that had evolved over millions of years faced introduced predators and loss of habitat as more forests were burnt, land cleared and wetlands drained. Charles Fleming, a leading scientist and conservationist, wrote in 1962 that the simplest explanation for all recent extinctions was that they were due to ecological changes caused by 'the arrival of man with fire, rats and dogs'.

The scientist Paul Callaghan gave his last public speech on 13 February 2012. He said that it was our wildlife that marks us out as unique in the world, and spoke about his 'moonshot' vision for a predator-free New Zealand:

> Let's get rid of the lot. Let's get rid of all the predators, all the damn mustelids, all the rats, all the possums, from the mainland islands of New Zealand ... It can be done, it's crazy, it's ambitious and I think it might be worth a shot, I think it's our great challenge, we should be the country that achieves the seemingly impossible.

INDEX